UNCLE RICO'S ENCORE

MOSTLY TRUE
STORIES OF
FILIPINO SEATTLE

PETER BACHO

UNIVERSITY OF WASHINGTON PRESS

Seattle

Uncle Rico's Encore was made possible in part by a grant from the Shawn Wong Book Fund, which supports the publication of books on Asian American history and culture.

Design by Laura Shaw Design
Composed in Alkes, typeface designed by Plamen Motev, Nikolay Petroussenko, and Kaja Słojewska; and Tolyer, typeface designed by Chatnarong Jingsuphatada.

26 25 24 23 22   5 4 3 2 1

Frontispiece: The author and family in front of their house on 32nd Avenue East (1962). Photo courtesy of the author.

UNIVERSITY OF WASHINGTON PRESS
uwapress.uw.edu

LIBRARY OF CONGRESS CATALOGING-IN-PUBLICATION DATA
Names: Bacho, Peter, author.
Title: Uncle Rico's encore : mostly true stories of Filipino Seattle / Peter Bacho.
Description: Seattle : University of Washington Press, [2022]
Identifiers: LCCN 2021015306 (print) | LCCN 2021015307 (ebook) |
ISBN 9780295749778 (hardcover; acid-free paper) |
ISBN 9780295749785 (ebook)
Subjects: LCSH: Bacho, Peter. | Filipino American authors—20th century—
Biography. | Filipino Americans—Biography. | LCGFT: Autobiographies.
Classification: LCC PS3552.A2573 Z46 2021 (print) |
LCC PS3552.A2573 (ebook) | DDC 813/.54 [B]—dc23
LC record available at https://lccn.loc.gov/2021015306
LC ebook record available at https://lccn.loc.gov/2021015307

♾ This paper meets the requirements of ANSI/NISO Z39.48-1992
(Permanence of Paper).

CONTENTS

ON BOXING, MOTHER, VIOLENCE, AND WRITING

A CLOSE CALL, MEMORIES, A LAST GOODBYE

ACKNOWLEDGMENTS

I would like to thank my editor at the University of Washington Press, Mike Baccam, and my wife, Mary, for reading each story and consistently providing insight, timely suggestions, and sound advice. Thanks also to my old friend James Charles McKay, who was my sounding board on the old Seattle that we both knew and loved. Finally, I would like to thank the Seattle Pinoys of the first and second generations. They lived, and many are still living, lives well worth writing about.

UNCLE RICO'S ENCORE

INTRODUCTION

T he idea for this collection came to me on my sixty-eighth birthday, a time of pause and recollection and an occasional barb. ("Hoy, old goat, you don't look a day over sixty-seven.")

Exactly fifty years earlier, on my eighteenth birthday, for several hours I would stand, sit, write, and bend over in the old army induction center on the west side of Queen Anne Hill in Seattle. What happened there on that day would change the course of my life.

I hadn't written in years, and I was pleased with my mini-memoir, "September 20, 1968." Other small pieces followed, not immediately—I had no book contract deadline to worry about—but over time, when I couldn't shake a memory of Seattle, my hometown, or Chinatown and the Central Area, or my parents or my mom's stories, or my uncles and cousins and a host of close friends.

My Pinoy friends and I had a lot in common. We were poor or blue collar and American born; most of us lived in the Central Area or South End, both working-class, multi-ethnic neighborhoods; some of us lived in the projects, and some of us ran the streets and were quick with our tempers, quick with our fists. English was our first, and typically our only, language.

All of us had Filipino fathers; not all of us had Filipino mothers. That was no big deal; to us, racial purity didn't matter. We were Pinoys, the bottom line.

Our parents, our fathers in particular, had come to this new land in the 1920s and 1930s. They arrived just in time for the Depression and the violent anti-Filipino racism up and down the West Coast, where most of them settled. Our fathers and uncles lived much of their lives in the margins, working dead-end, often backbreaking jobs in California fields and Alaska salmon canneries. The luckier ones cooked or washed dishes in restaurant kitchens in Seattle, Stockton, and Los Angeles.

My friends and I knew their stories of racial hostility and violence.

But we also knew the stories of resistance, of how they formed militant labor unions to demand higher wages and better working conditions. Certainly that was the case in 1965, when Larry Itliong led Filipino grape pickers off the fields in Delano, California. The Pinoys were later joined by Mexican workers led by the iconic Cesar Chavez. Together the two groups formed the United Farm Workers and launched the famed strike and grape boycott that same year.

But for me, the most successful example of Filipino resistance can be found in the history of Local 37 of the International Longshoremen's and Warehousemen's Union (the ILWU). Every spring, Seattle-based Local 37 would dispatch thousands of migrant workers, mostly Filipinos, to the Alaska salmon canneries.

In the 1950s, during the height of the McCarthy era, the union was led by a Communist, my friend Chris Mensalvas. For the federal government that was a problem.

This was the poisonous paranoid time of Senator Joseph McCarthy, who rose to prominence by playing on America's Cold War fears and providing simple answers in a post–World War II world that was increasingly complex and rapidly changing. McCarthy falsely declared that America was riddled with Communists and fellow travelers and that these "traitors"—professors, government officials, Hollywood writers, union officials, liberals—were corroding the nation from within. And he had lists of names to prove it.

For McCarthy and his ilk, half-truths and lies were his cudgels of choice. Conformity became the rule, and political dissent became treason.

Readers should now close their eyes and imagine the irony: a Filipino Communist leading a major union during the McCarthy era.

Despite the enormous pressure placed on the union by the federal government, Local 37 did not break or give up its leader. Mensalvas remained president until 1959, five years after McCarthy was censured by the Senate and two years after McCarthy's death in 1957.

By any standard, this is a remarkable example of ferocious defiance, largely untold and unknown, but remarkable nonetheless. I tell the tale of Local 37 in "Bad Attitude," which is included in this story collection. What led these old Pinoys to act as they did, when other Americans were rolling over and naming names? Over the years I've pondered this question, and I think I have some answers.

The Filipinos of my dad's era were an especially tough bunch. All had experienced racism and hardship, many had joined militant labor unions, many had survived combat. Years of adversity helped to build backbone—their intense pride, their edgy, don't-mess-with-me attitude—and a powerful sense of community. These were distinctive features that marked my father's generation and allowed them to survive in this new and often hostile land. For them, the union's fight with the federal government was just another enemy to confront—and overcome.

I would like to think that some of those traits have been passed on and absorbed by us, their American-born sons and daughters. Our parents' legacy—that sense of community—is what we inherited. And the bonds that we built over more than fifty years still remain strong.

But not all of the stories in this collection are as dramatic as Local 37's stand against the federal government. In fact, most of these stories are devoid of political meaning and historic import, and instead are accounts of smaller, more intimate memories—of losing a mother, of remembering her stories and pretending to enjoy her bland, untasty meals; of losing an uncle and losing good friends; of losing a marriage; of almost losing my life.

The longer I live, the more I will lose. That's life.

But each morning when I rise, I pause to remember the preciousness of what I have lost, and I cherish it. That's also life.

The old Pinoy community of my youth and memory is gone, dispersed by change and movement and the passing of time. Today there are still Filipinos in Seattle, thousands more in fact. But many of them arrived after 1968, when US immigration laws were loosened. Unlike my parents' generation, many of these newer arrivals came with college degrees and professional credentials and landed on a much softer spot in a kinder time in the new land.

I am sure that they or their children or grandchildren have their own stories to tell.

This collection tells mine.

THE LAY OF
THE LAND

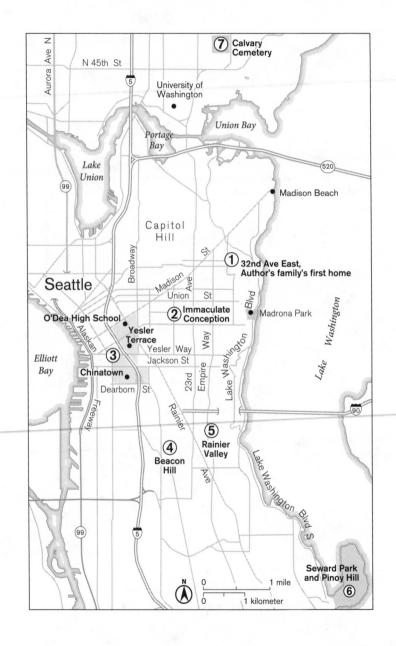

MAP 1

———

I n my dreams, sometimes there's a map of the city I love.
In almost seventy years not much has changed. And
that gives me comfort.

On this map I follow the lines—north, south, east, west—
and find the intersection, 32nd Avenue East and Thomas.
This is where my family used to live, in a small one-floor
yellow house that is still standing. The location is the eastern edge of the Central Area, the historic home of Seattle's
African American community, or so the tagline goes. But
the Central Area was also home to Filipinos, working-class
whites, and other ethnic groups.

On our side, the eastern side of the block, there was
another Filipino family (the Berganos), a Japanese American family, and three Black families. Across the street lived
an older white couple, Al and Olga Castle.

———

Facing page: Seattle, 1968. Circled numbers refer to "map" stories in this
book. *Map by Pease Press.*

As a kid, I loved our house and our block. I felt safe there, protected. I had doting parents, good friends, and enough to eat. In my twenty years of living on our stretch of 32nd, I don't recall the cops ever having been called.

As an adult watching our nation go through powerful, earth-shifting racial convulsions, I love that house, that neighborhood, that street even more.

I would leave that little house, fishing pole in hand, to join neighborhood pals for bike rides or hikes to the lake or the Arboretum lagoon, or I would leave with my bat and mitt for Little League practice in Washington Park.

And sometimes, especially during the summer, I would leave with a darker purpose—to ambush drivers heading northbound on 32nd Avenue East with my friends, a motley, multiracial gang of vandals in the making.

We would lie prone, hidden and still in the uncut grass, our peashooters at the ready. Then we'd inhale, hold our breath, and ping cars as they drove north in the far lane. It was all great fun until one afternoon, we hit a driver who'd left his window open. The peas flew and hit him upside his head.

The red '56 Chevy screeched to a halt. A young white man opened the car door and started running toward us. "You little motherfuckers!" he screamed.

We scattered, running through backyards, jumping fences, and disappearing into the woods. After several minutes of hiding in the trees and behind blackberry bushes, we eventually reemerged. I bumped into Allan Bergano, my friend, neighbor, and pea-shooting dead eye.

Allan was worried. "Do you think he'll go to our homes and tell our parents?"

I shrugged. "Mine are out shoppin'." I walked a few steps, then stopped. "What's a 'motherfucker'?" I asked.

✦

Although it's been more than half a century since I've been inside our old house, I remember minute details of each room, closet, and nook as if I had visited yesterday. Most of my memories of where we lived are comforting and warm.

But not all.

Like late one night when I was eight, I woke up to the shape of a woman standing at the foot of my brother's bed. I blinked, at first unbelieving and unsure, hoping I wasn't seeing what I was seeing. I took a deep breath, then closed my eyes and opened them again.

I gulped. I was seeing what I was seeing. She was translucent and her hands were joined together, fingers pointing up as if in prayer. She didn't move or speak. I didn't think she was evil—a small comfort—but I was still terrified. Worse, I had to pee, and she didn't seem to be in any rush to leave.

But I didn't want to get up and draw attention to myself. Having her float after me through the room, down the hall, and to the bathroom—uh, no thanks. Nor did I turn on the lamp on my bedside table, figuring that if the light went on and she was still there, I could be in trouble.

"Dear Jesus," I whispered. "Help me."

My fear was exhausting, and at some point I either fainted or fell asleep. To this day, I'm not sure which. When I came to or awoke the next morning, she was gone. I quickly scanned the room, then jumped out of bed and raced to the door.

I still had to pee.

As I look back, I've come to conclude that the ghost's visit was really a blessing. It was the first episode of a life full of moments I cannot explain. It has left me open to the inexplicable, to an ongoing and deep sense of wonder and surprise. From that point on, I have avoided certitudes and writ-in-stone, unbending dogmas, never once claiming that I now have all the answers—this is why things happen, trust me, I've figured it out.

And then there was the time when I was nine and a Catholic priest molested me. I came home one day after school, and there at the table sat this odd-looking child-sized Filipino man. He was sipping a Coke and chatting with Mom in Bisayan, laughing at everything she said.

I'd never heard a priest laugh, at least not the white ones I knew. Maybe they weren't supposed to. And I'd never seen a Filipino priest, but there he was in his miniature black uniform complete with white collar.

"Hoy, Peter," Mom said. "This is Father Veronico. He's from Cebu, and he's visiting the archdiocese. He's our guest tonight."

I just stood there, unable to stop staring at this strange little man.

Mom nodded her head. "*Psst*, don't be rude. Come here and introduce yourself."

I walked two steps toward him, stopped, and extended my right hand.

Veronico reached forward and grabbed me, pulling me in. "Nice boy," he said, giggling as he hugged me tightly. "Nice boy."

I went limp.

✦

I was in my pajamas and lying in my bed when Veronico walked in. He was beaming, giggling, and holding in his tiny hand a black rosary.

"Your mother says you pray," he said.

"Yes, Father, but I've already prayed."

Veronico looked at me sternly. "My son, you can never pray enough," he said, as he slipped in bed beside me. "Our Father," he began, as he placed a hand on my groin.

"Who art in heaven," I dutifully replied, as his short fingers started massaging me.

And so it went. We finished the rosary, and he left the room. I turned over on my side and fell asleep.

✦

More than sixty years later, my initial reaction to this incident puzzles me. Unlike other victims of sexual predation, I had no recurring nightmares, no suicidal thoughts, no feelings of guilt or shame or violation. For me, it was just an odd moment with a strange little man. It happened. I moved on and never told Mom or Dad.

But over the years, I think I've found an answer. Because of my mom, ours was a deeply religious home. Sex, as far as I can remember, was never mentioned or ever done within these walls. In our impenetrable sex-free bubble, people did not do what people do.

In my nine-year-old world, sex and sexual monsters did not exist. After all, Mary, a virgin, gave birth to Jesus. Did it happen again when my sister Irma was born? I had no clue as to how that came about. At age nine I was asexual, an innocent. And that invincible Catholic innocence, I am now convinced, is what saved me from the residue of Veronico's heinous crime and sin.

Years later I was in Seattle visiting Mom. She was at the stove, tending to an almost done chicken adobo. I was sitting at the kitchen table, enjoying the fragrance, sipping coffee, and reading the newspaper. Then a headline caught my eye: "Pedophile Lawsuit Rocks Archdiocese." My heart started to race, and I put the paper down.

"Mom, whatever happened to that priest?" I casually asked.

"Which one?" she said without turning around.

"That little guy from Cebu."

"Oh, Father Veronico."

"Yeah, Father short-eyes himself," I mumbled.

"Short-eyes?"

"Oh nothing, Mom, nothing."

"Not sure. We lost contact, but I got a Christmas card from him a few years ago when you were still in California." She hovered over the pot, dipped a spoon, and sampled the sauce. "Almost done," she said with her back still turned, as she added a pinch of salt.

"Oh, so what did he say?"

"Who?"

"Veronico."

"He says he's well and is in charge of an orphanage in Cebu City."

"Oh?"

"He says he loves his job."

"I'll bet." I turned to the side. "Burn in hell," I whispered. "You motherfucker."

Mom turned around. She was smiling. "The adobo, son. It's ready."

MAP 2

n my dream my focus shifts west, and I am walking the downward slope of Union Street, the corridor that connects the Central Area to downtown and, beyond, Puget Sound. In short order, I cross Empire Way, then 23rd Avenue, where I pass a grocery store to my left where my parents used to shop and across 23rd, the second-floor office of my dentist, Dr. Browning.

As an adult, I have avoided dentists for decades, preferring instead to let bad, aging teeth fall out of my mouth. *As nature intended*, I tell myself.

But as a child, I liked going to Dr. Browning. As I recall, he was a tall, powerful, physically imposing man—David "Deacon" Jones without the helmet and dressed in white. But with me he was very gentle and skilled—and the only Black dentist I have ever known.

One time he removed a loose tooth while chatting casually about baseball, my favorite sport. I nervously sat in his dentist's chair, my fists clenched, my mouth wide open, my eyes shut tight, praying.

"So, son, let me guess," he began. "Your favorite player is . . ." He then bent over, peering into my mouth. "Hmm," I heard him say, before he inserted his forefinger and thumb. "Willie Mays," he said casually.

I nodded.

He handed me the tooth. "Mine, too."

"I'm done?" I asked.

He smiled. "Yes," he said, patting me on the head. "You're a good boy."

I didn't feel a thing.

✦

This is a walk I have done many times, especially in the warm afternoon days of late spring, summer, and early fall. I am walking for more than an hour, but I am young, sixteen, and wearing my white Converse high-tops. I never tire, never sweat, or even break stride.

But that was then, and such a long time ago. Today, I can only walk this walk in my dreams.

I turn left, heading south on 18th Avenue, and I see my destination: the distinctive twin spires of Immaculate Conception, the pulsing heart of old Pinoy Seattle. In those days, Immaculate was a church, a grade school, and a high school for girls. A lot of Filipinos were parishioners and students.

In front of the church, I see Annie, a young Pinay, who lives across the street. We stop to chat.

"Where ya goin'?" she asks.

"Catch me a game or two." In the background, I can hear the telltale siren sounds: a hard quick dribble and someone shouting, "Hey, man, I was open. I was open . . . Damn."

Immaculate Conception Church. Photo by Joe Mabel.

"Gotta go," I tell Annie as I jog toward the parking lot and its outdoor hoop. "Got me an itch I gotta go scratch." I am in the parking lot behind the church, resting against the fence by the basket and watching a three-on-three, shirts versus skins half-court game. I know all of the players:

all Filipinos, all friends. They aren't that tall and some aren't especially skilled, not like the lean, long-limbed brothers at Madrona who have sports page clippings, college scholarship offers, and citywide reputations. No matter. They're ballers who do their best and love playing the game.

I'm at Immaculate that afternoon because at sixteen, I will roam the city each day on foot or by bus looking for a game. For my younger self, basketball is my only focus, my addiction; playing it is the only thing that matters.

I'd thought about going to Madrona, but the games there are so intense, such intensely physical chest-to-back, hand-to-hand battles, and today I just don't have the energy to compete. Maybe tomorrow will be different. But for now at least, I'm on vacation, enjoying a rare, relaxed Madronaless basketball day.

But there's another reason I'm here: Today I just feel like being with other Pinoys.

The game is near the end. The score is tied, fourteen all. A bucket by either side ends it, and the winners keep playing. The ball moves quickly, from the corner to Alan at the top of the key. He head fakes his defender, gets him off balance, then shoots an open jumper. The ball bounces twice, then hangs on the rim before going in.

Game over. The winners smile and nod their heads.

"Sweet," Tony, an older player, says, clenching his fist. "Dat's what I'm talkin' 'bout, fellas." He walks to the fence, pulls a pack of Salems from his jacket pocket, and lights up a smoke. That's something you wouldn't see at Madrona.

I nod at Tony, then raise my hand. "I got next."

My good friend Bob, who is on the losing side, walks over and hands me the ball. For a moment I hold it, then dribble it low, hard, and fast. The texture of the ball, the bounce, they all feel good.

"Hey, man," Bob says. "Great to see you."

We shake hands. I give him a hug. "Damn good to be here," I say.

✦

The Flors belonged to Immaculate Conception parish. Same with the Lunas, the Israels, the Galarosas, the Ragudoses, the Delmas, the Ogilvies, the Farrells, the Villaflors, the Beltrans, and a long list of others. I stay in touch with many of them.

Over the years hundreds of Pinoys were baptized and confirmed in this dark, cavernous church. It's where many of us took our first communion and confessed our sins, where we joined in marriage and mourned our dead.

Immaculate was also the spiritual home of the late Fred Cordova. He and his wife, Dorothy, are two Pinoy legends. They are also among the best human beings I have ever known. In 1957 they founded Filipino Youth Activities, which sponsored sports teams, classes on Filipino culture, deep discussions on Filipino history and identity, and in 1959 an award-winning drill team that, more than sixty years later, still rocks the show at Seattle's famed Torchlight Parade.

As a kid attending the Torchlight and other summer parades, I loved watching the FYA drill team. I still do.

Da-da . . . da, two quick beats followed by a paused third: these were the signature rhythmic sounds of the ends of bamboo sticks hitting pavement. Then came Fred's whistle, the clanging of a cowbell, and the pulsing Latin and Moro drumbeats of the percussioneers. The drill team was heard first, then seen. This has not changed.

When they passed me I was focused, excited. I loved the precision, the elegance, the head-tilting, jaw-jutting arrogance of the girls in their long red dresses keeping time with their sticks and the focus of the boys pounding beats in their black slacks and green tunics. I loved hearing the applause and whistles from onlookers. I loved hearing the *oohs*. I was proud of the drill team and all that it represented.

When Fred died in 2014, the funeral at Immaculate was packed, standing-room only, a fitting testament to his life. His death was a devastating loss to his family. But it was a loss to us as well.

His body lay in an open casket. I bent over and kissed his forehead.

Fred was wearing the jersey of his favorite Seahawk, Doug Baldwin, who is Filipino on his mother's side. Of course.

I walked over to console Dorothy. "Fred loved you," she whispered.

"I know. I loved him, too."

Later, I wrote to a friend. "He made it easy for me to be a young Filipino in Seattle."

I was not the only one.

MAP 3

---

am now standing on Terry Avenue, in front of O'Dea, the all-male Catholic high school I am attending. A lot of Pinoys attend O'Dea, some following in the footsteps of older brothers and cousins, uncles and fathers.

It is a worthy tradition.

The Irish Christian Brothers do a very good job of educating poor and working-class boys, giving us the skills to succeed in college or whatever path we will choose. Biology is a required class, the same with Latin, algebra, calculus, and chemistry. From us the Brothers always demand the best; they cajole, encourage, and threaten us with grievous bodily harm.

They never accept excuses.

My Black and Filipino peers do well at O'Dea. For us, going to college isn't just a wisp of smoke from an opium pipe dream.

O'Dea High School. Photo by Joe Mabel.

That isn't so at Seattle's public high schools, where racial stereotypes are pervasive, and indifferent teachers and counselors just go through the motions, allowing boys of these colors to slip through the cracks. For too many of my friends, it was high school and done, which in those days meant the draft, the army, and basic training at eighteen, then at nineteen, Vietnam. Their dreams weren't crushed; they weren't even born.

More than half a century later, I still carry a grudge against Seattle Public Schools. And I still thank my parents for sending me to O'Dea.

In senior year, I remember talking to my friend Mike, the center on our basketball team. The fierce determination, intelligence, and discipline so apparent on the court he also applied in the classroom. Unlike me, he understood math. Unlike me, he excelled at science. I asked Mike what he wanted to be after graduation.

"A Black brain," he said evenly, without the trace of a smile, a moment of doubt, or slight hesitation.

Damn, I love this school.

From Terry, I walk west to Eighth Avenue, then turn left and head south. My destination is King Street in Chinatown, and my route takes me past Harborview Medical Center and through the heart of Yesler Terrace, one of the city's public housing projects, where lucky west-side tenants enjoy a stunning view of downtown, Puget Sound, and the majestic snow-capped Olympic Mountains.

Today, Yesler Terrace is no longer the same. It now has a mix of subsidized and market-rate apartments. The old project has been "redeveloped," which means spending millions of dollars to move a lot of rich folk in and a lot of poor folk out. A priceless view, after all, should never be squandered on the poor.

But in 1967, Yesler is home to a lot of Filipinos, including my good friend Jesse and the alluring Dolores, a beautiful brown-eyed Filipino-Mexican girl and my high school crush.

One Friday afternoon, after I had graduated, Dolores and I were sitting in the bleachers at Broadway Playfield, relaxing, enjoying the early September sun, and chatting casually about school and movies, normal kid things. The year before, she was my date for the senior prom. Since then we would sometimes stay in touch, and I could never stop thinking about her. But I eventually stopped calling and drifted away, mostly because I wasn't sure what to do next.

Our meeting that day was happenstance, proof to me that God loves fools. We'd bumped into each other on a nearby street and decided to walk to the playfield, sit in the bleachers, and catch up. Dolores was still in her blue Immaculate Conception uniform. As she spoke, I smiled and nodded and discreetly admired her brown, exquisitely formed seventeen-year-old calves.

I was nineteen at the time—still a confession-going, guilt-eating virgin—and what little I could see was all I could imagine. At that age I had never seen, much less touched, a female nipple. I was a mess and living a pitiful existence, a nippleless life.

Her calves would have to do.

We were together again. On that afternoon, that's all that mattered.

"Let's go to Vancouver," I blurted out of the blue.

Dolores smiled. "BC?"

"Yup."

"Sure, when?" She paused.

I gulped. "Tomorrow," I said, without figuring out how I'd scrape up the money, or whether my hand-me-down Mercury Meteor could get us to Vancouver, or, more important, what we'd do when we got there. But this deal, which had come out of nowhere, was now on the table. I had to seal it.

"Tomorrow's Saturday, so we can leave early in the morning," I said, trying to sound confident, like this was no big deal, something I did all the time.

"You can make up a story. Your mom's workin' early, right? Tell her you'll be spending the night with a girlfriend, leave her a note. Tell her don't worry . . . ah, I dunno. Somethin'." I looked at her. She was smiling.

"I'd love to see Vancouver," she said. "I've seen pictures, and it's very pretty."

Damn, I thought, *she's actually willing to go*. My heart started racing. I could feel my face redden, so I turned away, hoping she wouldn't notice, and took a deep breath.

I turned to face her. "Why not?" I added casually.

Dolores called the next day. Something had come up, she explained. After all these years, the details have become hazy. But I think her boyfriend objected.

We never took the trip. To this day, I wish we had.

I cross Yesler Street and make my way to the path leading down to Jackson Street and Chinatown. Once across Jackson, I pass the Jun Fan Gung Fu Institute on Eighth Avenue. The institute itself is bare and nondescript, two large empty rooms in a dusty basement. But it was founded by a legend, Bruce Lee, who'd already moved to Los Angeles and had left the school in the care of his trusted friend and student Taky Kimura.

I'd never met Bruce, but I saw him on several episodes of *The Green Hornet* thanks to a Pinoy pal Steve, who gave me a heads-up.

"Man," he said, his tone low, reverential. "I'm tellin' ya, he's somethin' else. Explosive. You just gotta check this dude out."

So I did, and, suitably impressed, I joined the school two weeks ago, training when I can during the week. But today is Saturday. The school is closed, and I keep walking.

At the corner of Eighth and King I stop and pull the neck of my T-shirt up to cover my mouth and nose. The shit and blood stench from the live chicken market a few blocks east is especially bad on this hot, early August, dead-air afternoon.

"Chinatown, only in Chinatown," I grumble, as I turn right on King and head west. Two blocks later, I reach my destination: Tai Tung, the city's oldest Chinese restaurant. When Bruce lived in Seattle, he used to eat here.

My Uncle Rico and I are eating here today.

✦

I had called my uncle earlier that day, asking if he was free for lunch. Of course, he is. He's retired.

Today is a rarity: For once, I have some extra cash from some odd jobs. Plus, my focus on basketball means I hadn't seen him for a couple of months.

When I was four or so, my greatest fear was that my dad, my Uncle Vic, and their cousin Quirico Daan would die too soon. These were men I admired and loved. I wanted them to live long lives and never leave me, but the math was bad. Dad was in his mid-forties when I was born, or about twenty years older than the fathers of most of my friends. And Vic and Rico were about the same age.

Today I am missing my uncle. It is time to reconnect.

I enter the restaurant and spot him sipping tea in a corner booth. A waiter had just delivered a bowl of white rice and plates of sweet-and-sour pork and shrimp chow mein, staples of our countless lunches together.

I know now it wasn't very imaginative, daring fare, but I was just a kid. No Asian fusion, no fussy newspaper critiques, no MSG ban, no this, no that. But to my unsophisticated teenage taste buds, the grub tasted good. So why change?

I walk over to kiss him on the top of his head.

"Hoy, long time, boy," he says, as I slide into the booth.

"Sorry, Uncle," I say. "Been playin' ball all summer and . . ."

"You good now?"

"Better," I say, as I scoop some rice and put it on my plate.

"I gonna go watch you play, okay?" he says.

I smile. "Okay," I say. "I'd like that."

We continue eating and say very little. It's always been this way. His English is bad; my Bisayan is worse, but we've never needed a translator. That's just how we are. I like being around him, and I know he feels the same about me.

At the end of the meal, I signal for the check and pull out my wallet. Rico frowns, shakes his head, and waves his hand.

"No," he says.

"Too late, Uncle," I say, as I hand the waiter a twenty.

He shrugs. "So, you got girlfriend now?"

"Nah, too busy," I say. "Basketball, you know. Who knows. But maybe after the season. Too busy right now." I pause. "How 'bout you?"

"Blondie," he says.

"A blonde?"

He giggles.

"That's cuz you're so damn guapo," I say.

He giggles again.

✦

After lunch, I walk west toward Union Station. It's been a while since I've been in this part of Chinatown, and I walk slowly partly because it's hot but mostly because I want to stop and smell the scents of boiling rice and of garlic, vinegar, and ginger wafting through open windows and doors. I want to absorb it all.

I also want to savor the memories of my childhood, of good times past: of hundreds of Pinoys gathering each spring awaiting dispatch to Alaska, laughing and talking loud and renewing old friendships. Then the fall Chinese dinner celebrations upon their return. And year-round, the hotel room visits with friends and relatives, the lunches and dinners at Tai Tung and other Cantonese joints.

I walk by the post office and then reach the Victory Bath House. I glance inside and see a group of old Pinoys playing cards, just like my dad and uncles used to do. I recognize all of their faces but can't remember all of their names.

One of them looks up and smiles. "Hoy, youngster, how's your dad?" he asks.

I smile back. "Fine," I say.

"Tell him Marcelino says hi. We worked in Alaska together way back in the old days," he says, before throwing down his cards. "Cocksucker," he grunts.

"I will, manong," I say.

My next stop is the barber shop across the alley run by a kind and very old Japanese woman who lived in the back of the shop. My folks used to take me there twice a month for a haircut. No one was sure what her name was. We just called her Mama San.

The sign on the door says "closed," so I peer through the plate glass window and see two red barber chairs. On the two walls facing each other are two wall-length mirrors. I used to sit in the chair and stare at my image—endlessly replicating, endlessly shrinking. I was fascinated.

"Mama," I once asked her, "does it ever end?"

"What?"

"Me in this chair."

She looked at the reflection of me in the mirror and laughed softly. "No, I don't think so."

I didn't know it then, but a barber chair, two mirrors, and an old Japanese woman had introduced me to eternity.

✦

I reach the corner of King Street and Fifth Avenue South, the western edge of Chinatown. I'll soon be turning back, but before I do, I pause, wipe my brow, and catch my breath. Across the street an old Pinoy is leaving the Publix Lunch, where years ago my folks and I would sit at the counter, and Mom would order three hamburger patties on Wonder Bread.

I recognize him and wave. It's Filemon, my mom's cousin, and one of my favorites.

"Hi, Uncle Phil," I say. He waves back. I cross the street and give him a hug. "What're you doin' in town?"

"Back from Alaska this morning," he says. "Short season, not much fish. Was about to call your folks. Gonna leave Monday for LA."

Uncle Phil steps back and looks at me. He nods his approval and grabs me by the elbow. "Hey, you growin' tall now," he says. "You hungry?"

"No, I just . . . never mind," I say, then pause. "Sure, sure, I'm up for a bite."

He smiles and opens the door. I follow him in, and we sit at the counter. The waitress, a fifty-something white woman, comes over and looks at Uncle Phil, her pen at the ready. I think I remember her.

"Whatcha have, hon?"

"Black Label," he says. "No ice."

She turns to me. "Hmm, let me guess," she says. "Hamburger patty on Wonder Bread." She smiles.

"Of course," I say. "Of course."

MAP 4

———

The rest of 1967 is a blur—my senior year at O'Dea, basketball season, college plans, and, if I luck out and play well enough, maybe even a basketball scholarship. Then the blur continues to 1968, with the Tet Offensive in Vietnam, huge protests against a war that won't end, Senator Eugene McCarthy's almost successful primary challenge to Lyndon Johnson, and the president, looking tired, and saying *basta* on national television.

"I shall not seek, and I will not accept, the nomination of my party for another term as your president," Johnson said. I watched the broadcast, and I was stunned, speechless. LBJ has had enough. He will be stepping down.

The murders of Martin Luther King Jr. and Bobby Kennedy soon follow, as do race riots in major American cities, and a cop riot at the Democratic National Convention in Chicago. Black people are demanding. White people are resenting.

I am almost eighteen, almost draft bait, and thousands of my young fellow Americans are dying in faraway rice paddies, jungles, and swamps. Others are losing their minds.

"Man, it's all gone crazy," my Pinoy friend Eddie says.

I nod, shaking my head.

He opens his jacket to show a snubnosed revolver in a shoulder holster. Eddie is street savvy and tough, very fast and quick with his fists. But in 1968, even he's taking no chances.

"This baby here's for just in case some fool tries to go crazy," he says. "If I'm goin', I ain't goin' alone." He zips up his jacket. "Nowadays, I don't never leave home without it."

Eddie looks at me steely-eyed, serious. It is a look that shrinks the will of those he's about to fight. "Hey man," he says, "you should get you one of these."

"I'll think about it."

Welcome to adulthood. Welcome to 1968. Welcome also to the Chinese curse, "May you live in interesting times."

But I don't deserve this curse. I didn't start the war in Vietnam. I didn't make this damn, screwed-up world. I didn't make the chaos. I just have to figure out how to survive it.

During these months I am distracted, afraid, confused. Through it all, I continue to dream. But now there are only nightmares—of me face down in a rice paddy, of me in a body bag and my mother wailing, of me back home in a wheelchair, and worst of all, of me losing it in combat.

I do not, cannot, dream the map of Pinoy Seattle.

Then, one night in late summer, I am asleep, dreaming once again, but this time the map, like an old and long gone friend, suddenly reappears.

In my dream I am now walking east on King Street, leaving Chinatown. And as I near the live chicken market,

I hold my breath until I reach 12th Avenue South. I finally exhale and can feel the breeze blowing east to west, taking the stench away from the direction I'm heading. At 12th, I take a right and start walking south toward Beacon Hill.

In my dream I am crossing a nondescript city bridge.

I don't know it at the time, but in 1974 it will bear the name of Jose Rizal, the martyred national hero of the Philippines. Just beyond the bridge and up a hill will be a large public park with a panoramic view of the city. It, too, will be named after Rizal.

Jose Rizal in Seattle? What the hell's he doing here?

The story of how this came to be is worth retelling. In the 1890s Rizal's biting political novels and other writings helped trigger the Filipino revolution against Spain, the Philippines' colonial overlord. There's no doubt that Rizal was an admirable man—brilliant, eloquent, principled, and brave—but what he did those decades ago in the land of my parents matters little to me and my American-born, English-speaking peers.

Our yawning indifference to the Philippines' national hero wasn't the case with my Uncle Vic, Dad's brother, and the men and women of their generation. To them, Jose Rizal mattered. Many, like Uncle Vic, were born less than a decade after Rizal died. He became their symbol of dignity in a new land that had quickly crushed their hopes and rejected them.

In the 1920s Uncle Vic and Trinidad Rojo had come to America to attend college. In 1973 they began lobbying city officials to rename a Seattle street, any street, to honor Rizal. Despite their age—both were in their seventies—the memories of those bitter times pushed them forward.

The author's parents at a political function/dinner at the Olympic Hotel in Seattle, circa 1960. Photo courtesy of the author.

Local elected officials with Filipino community leaders standing at the head table, Olympic Hotel, circa 1960. Photo courtesy of the author.

For Uncle Vic the project had become an obsession. One afternoon, while I was at his house, I asked him why. At the time he was sitting at his desk, leafing through a pile of correspondence with different city officials.

"White people," he explained, without glancing up. "They have to respect us." He looked at me, his face solemn and sad.

"Have you ever been called a monkey?"

"No."

"I have."

Both Trinidad and Uncle Vic were tireless and persistent, and they had the support of most of a growing, politically active Filipino community. In 1973 Seattle mayor Wes

Uncle Vic Bacho shaking hands with US senator Henry Jackson, circa
1960. Uncle Vic had extensive personal connections to influential
national and local politicians. Such connections and Uncle Vic's acute
understanding of American politics proved vital in making the Rizal
Bridge and Park project a reality. Photo courtesy of the author.

Former Seattle mayor Wes Uhlman at a meet and greet, circa 1972, hosted by Uncle Vic at his Northeast Seattle home. The author's mother, Reme, is standing to the right. Photo courtesy of the author.

Uhlman suggested the bridge and an undeveloped plot of land just south of the bridge as a candidate. In 1974 the city held a rededication ceremony, proclaiming that the bridge and the yet-to-be-built park would both bear Rizal's name.

Amazing, I thought at the time.

Amazing, I still think today.

✦

I am now on Beacon heading south, passing the Jefferson Park Golf Course on my left. I stop and watch an old out-of-shape duffer line up then miss a three-foot putt. He tosses his club, clenches his fists, tilts his head back, and screams.

Two men in his foursome turn away, trying hard not to laugh. The third makes a slashing sign with his fingers across his neck. "Choke," I can hear him say. I chuckle, then resume my walk.

My destination today is the Asa Mercer Junior High School gym, where I will play with a Pinoy team in an Asian American summer basketball league game. After O'Dea, I thought I was done with competitive ball. The scouts never came. I won't be playing in college.

I hadn't dribbled or shot a basketball in months. I'd stopped playing ball at Madrona; I'd stopped roaming the city looking for games. My jones for the sport was finally over, or so I told myself. It was time to move on.

But then my friend Larry calls. "We're formin' a team," he says. "You in?"

"Man, I ain't played in a while."

"Don't worry, it'll all come back."

I hesitate, unsure how much my skills have diminished. I used to be good, and I don't want to stumble around or embarrass myself. "Sure," I finally say. "Why not."

I go to the closet, bring out my Converse high-tops, brush off the dust, and lace them up. The shoes feel comfortable, supportive, snug.

To my surprise, the old passion comes back. Maybe it's the shoes. For this summer at least, I'm still good to go.

✦

I arrive at Mercer, and in the hall I can already hear the familiar welcome sounds of voices rising and basketballs being dribbled. I open the gym door and enter.

Our Japanese American opponents are warming up at one end, the Pinoys at the other. I look at my team. Something's different. Last week we had nine players. Today we're missing two.

I walk over to Kenny, shooting jumpers at the top of the key. The ball bounces back. I grab it and hand it to him.

He fakes twice, steps back, jumps, and releases the ball with a flick of his wrist. The motion is smooth, flawless, and I nod, knowing the result. Jerry West could not have done it better.

"That's two," I say, without turning to look. "Automatic. Sweet."

"Thanks," he says.

"Hey, Kenny," I ask, "where's John and Chick? You hear from 'em? Our roster today, it's lookin' kinda thin." I pause. "They gonna show?"

"They got snatched, man," Kenny tells me, as he leaves the court to join our teammates, huddling by the bench. I follow.

"Whatcha mean?"

"They're in basic," he says.

"Basic?"

"As in basic training, US Army, destination, hmm, most probably Vietnam," he says evenly.

I take a deep breath and exhale. "Damn," I say, as my guts start to churn.

"I'm goin' next," he says calmly. "My papers say two more weeks here and then . . . whatever, who knows . . ." I don't respond.

"Know what that means?" he asks.

I shake my head.

"I got two more games, brother, that's my only focus," Kenny says. "And we're winnin' 'em both. I can control that, sure 'nough, the rest . . ."

In two months I'll be eighteen. I sigh and walk toward the huddle.

Welcome to adulthood, I think to myself. Welcome to 1968. Damn.

MAP 5

Another day, another dream.

I am walking east leaving Beacon Hill and am now in the Filipino-rich Rainier Valley, a blue-collar, multiethnic neighborhood. Japanese and Chinese Americans live there, the same with Blacks, Sephardic Jews, and Italians, who even have their own Catholic church, Our Lady of Mount Virgin. The Valley is also home to a lot of Filipino families: the Alcantaras, the Sumaoangs, the Quinteros, the Floreses, the Martins, the Santoses, the Descargars, the Navarros, the Dumlaos, the Mamons, and the Sibongas, among others.

I am now on Empire Way, walking south, passing Franklin High School on my left. Franklin is the alma mater of Hall of Fame third baseman Ron Santo and a recent Washington governor, Gary Locke, a Chinese American, class of 1968. Many of Seattle's Pinoy kids, my peers, are FHS students or grads. I have known them, and our families have known each other, for years.

Graduation from high school is for most a welcome rite of passage, a shining, memorable moment, and a time of joy. It is the starting point for the rest of life. But not after 1965; for us, this is not a normal time.

The war in Vietnam is raging, US casualties are mounting by the day, and the draft will soon be sucking up young men turning eighteen. Most of the Filipinos I know will not be going to college; no one I know is thinking of running for governor. That means they will not be getting life-saving four-year deferments and instead will become American soldiers and Marines.

Their sudden burden—their fears, apprehensions, and delayed aspirations—will be shared by those who love them. The returning Pinoy veterans, at least those from Seattle, are welcomed home by those they left behind. The name-calling, the shame-mongering, the cries of "baby killers" stinging the ears of other vets didn't happen, at least not among Filipinos in Seattle.

By the 1970s I have grown to hate the war and have come to conclude it is a disaster on all counts—another dark, disastrous, unnecessary chapter of American history. But whatever I think, whatever political or moral qualms I have, I keep them to myself. My friends were in the bush, making life and death decisions. I wasn't there.

One evening I am sitting at a Chinatown restaurant with Pete, who was badly wounded in Vietnam. He is still carrying metal fragments in his body.

Out of the blue he says, "You know, man, we had to fight 'em there, otherwise we'd be fightin' 'em here."

I shrug and hold my tongue. "Maybe," I manage to mumble. I don't argue because these vets are our friends and family members. They served their tours and turned in their weapons. The federal government will now finally leave them alone. And, thank God, they returned home. For us, this is the bottom line, the only thing that matters.

The draft hits Franklin High hard. Many of the Pinoy graduates will fight in Vietnam. Most return to live decent, meaningful lives. As far as I know, all are in their seventies and still alive—except one.

✦

Chick musters out of the army. He makes it home. But Vietnam follows him across the Pacific to Seattle and never leaves. The war has changed him. He is haunted. He is not and will never be the same.

The last time I'd seen him before he left for basic training was after an Asian American Summer League basketball game. Our Pinoy team had won. Chick had played well.

"You on it tonight, brother," I tell him after the game. "We gonna do it again next week same time." He sighs but is otherwise silent. "Right?"

Chick nods his head and manages a slight smile. "Yeah, sure," he mumbles.

And then he is gone. I didn't have a chance to say goodbye.

✦

In high school, I'd heard about Chick before I'd met him. At the time, I was a freshman at O'Dea and focused solely on sports and school, in that order. My friend Steve, who was far more social, would keep me up-to-date about the comings and goings of Chick and other young Filipinos.

"Man, last Friday all of us were at this party at Laurie's," Steve began. "And Chick did [fill in the blank]."

"Nah."

"Man, you missed it," Steve said.

I shrugged. In those days I missed a lot of things not connected to catching footballs, shooting basketballs, and trying to hit curves.

Among Pinoys my age, Chick had already made a name for himself. Before the war he could do it all. He wasn't very big, maybe 5'9" and 145 pounds, modest dimensions that are hardly intimidating. But he was lean and loose and dapper, confident and handsome, a smooth talker, a good athlete, and a very good musician.

He was also a great dancer. When I first met him, we were at a weekend teen dance, when Chick busted a classic James Brown move. He stepped away from his partner and skated across the floor, his right foot smoothly, furiously swiveling to the funk. Then he did the splits and sprang back up to skate some more.

But unlike James, Chick didn't sweat, not a drop of perspiration; not a single hair was out of place. The other dancers watched, many *oohing* and nodding approval. The slightest of smiles and the tilt of his head said no applause needed. Ladies and gents, this ain't no big deal. No big deal at all.

Chick epitomized cool, and I was impressed. He also ran the streets, and despite his modest size, when trouble came calling, he'd never back down. Chick had heart, more courage than sense. He was a good friend and a dangerous enemy, another trait that I admired.

So it was no surprise when I later learned he was serving in an airborne unit. He had become an elite soldier, and his tour would be spent fighting the war not behind the wire sitting in an office, as I hoped to do, sipping coffee and typing reports. It was also no surprise when I learned he'd been wounded. The only good news was that he'd soon be coming home.

✦

Chick and I hook up after he gets back. We'd grab a meal or a drink and just sit and chat about old times and future plans. During our visits I never ask him about the war. It is none of my business. One afternoon, we meet in a bar near the University of Washington, where I am teaching and he is recently enrolled.

"Man, this college stuff," he says. "I dunno."

"Chick, you can do it," I say calmly. Right now, my friend is stuck in a tree; I need to talk him down. "You bright enough. No doubt 'bout that."

"Damn, but it's been such a long time since Franklin, more than ten years, so long . . ." He looks away, then looks back at me. "You mean that? I mean, about me bein' bright."

"Yeah, I mean it," I say firmly. "And I ain't just blowin' smoke up your ass."

And I wasn't either. Over the years, I've come to appreciate just how smart and thoughtful Chick really is. Among my circle of young Pinoys, he may have been the best college prospect, the smartest of us all. But this talent was obscured by his other teenage traits and skills.

Going to Franklin didn't help. There the indifference of teachers and staff to streetwise, too-cool Pinoys means we'll tolerate you because we have to.

The time races by, and suddenly the three years are up. And now it's commencement, and the guest speaker says, "You've graduated. Congratulations, for what it's worth. But now, it's the end of the line. Sure, have your little celebrations, but get off now and face the world, whether you're ready to or not. And to those young men who didn't go to class and aren't going to college, hey, fellas, good luck."

✦

Over the years we would meet several more times. One meeting I remember was in a coffee shop on Capitol Hill in 1988 or 1989, I can't recall. We are sitting at a table just laughing and talkin' and catching up—a little on the Sonics, other Pinoys, a little on school, normal things. Then Chick suddenly points his right index finger to a small scar in his upper neck.

"See this?" he asks.

"Yeah."

"Vietnam," he says.

"I figured."

"Well, I'm just layin' in my hospital bed, and this colonel, a white guy, comes walkin' by. He stops and stares, then comes over to me and . . ." Chick takes a deep breath, then exhales. "And . . . he jams his thumb into my wound and then the motherfucker says, 'We don't treat gooks.'"

Chick looks away. I do, too.

"My scream brings the nurses who finally pull him off me, but man . . ."

I blink. This is hard to hear. There's nothing I can say.

"You know, I believed, I really did, at least at the start," he says. "But now I wonder . . . some things I did, that we did, in my mind, they're still there. All the time, man, they're all still there."

Chick falls silent. I look down and don't say a word. There's nothing I can say.

✦

That was the last time I saw Chick. In 1989, I leave for San Francisco for another job and don't return for seven years. During that time we lose touch and drift away. And when I do come home, I settle in Tacoma, thirty miles from Seattle.

I miss Chinatown. I miss my pals. But I don't have a choice: The smaller city has cheaper rent and is closer to work. I try calling Chick a couple of times. He calls back. We both miss each other. I settle into my new life.

On occasion, when I travel to Seattle, I visit with some of my Pinoy veteran friends. I ask if they'd seen Chick.

"Not for a while," Teddy says. "He doesn't come around much."

"How's he doin'?"

Teddy shrugs. "I dunno," he says softly. "His life, man, Chick didn't have it easy."

"I know."

Years pass, and during that time I think about calling him again, but I don't. It would be awkward. The planet has taken too many trips around the sun. Then, months later, Teddy tells me some bad news.

"Man, I heard Chick went to the VA for surgery."

"Is he okay?"

Teddy shakes his head. "He's in a wheelchair."

Later, I chat with others who also know Chick. "A botched job," one says. "No way he should have ended up this way."

I am furious, and for a moment I think, Just how much burden should one person bear? I guess Chick's sacrifice in Vietnam wasn't enough. The federal government had to add one more weight; it just couldn't leave him alone.

A few months pass, and I am again in Seattle. I bump into Tony, Chick's younger brother. We stop and chat.

"I'm sorry about Chick," I say.

"He'll make it," Tony says. "He's a fighter."

I nod. "A fighter. Yes, he is."

✦

Chick's fight ended in 2016, after a prolonged illness. I drive to Seattle to attend the ceremony honoring his life. I see lots of Filipinos, many of them longtime friends. On the tables are Chick's army insignias and photos of him in baseball and basketball uniforms, playing the sports he loved. This is the Chick I remember.

I listen to the heartfelt eulogies. Near the end, I say a few words myself.

I then leave and once outside, I take out a cigarette, pack the tip with sage, and light it. A thin trail of smoke drifts lazily upward.

"Rest well, Brother Chick," I say slowly. "Your style, intelligence, and courage—I admired all of it. Among us, when we were all much younger than we are today. You were a bright, shining star. I'll miss you. Buddy, you were one of the best."

MAP 6

————

I am now dreaming that I am in Southeast Seattle in Seward Park, perched on a bluff overlooking Lake Washington. On July 4, 1960, and for as long as I can remember, the bluff has always been the western side of Pinoy Hill.

But at ten years old, I'm not really sure why or how the hill got its one-day name. I later learn that July 4th is truly special. It isn't just an American holiday that the rest of the nation celebrates. It is also the date of Philippine independence from the United States.

Today in the early afternoon I am surrounded by maybe a thousand Filipinos from Seattle and beyond celebrating both events. I am standing with my sister Virginia, who is four years older. Our plan today is to go fishing in the lake down the hill and step away from the revelry. She is holding our fishing poles. I am holding a can of worms. I recognize most of the families. But some I don't know.

"Who's that?" I ask Virginia, pointing to a young couple holding hands and walking by us.

"I'm not sure," she says. "Must be from out of town, maybe Sumner or Renton."

My parents, cagey July 4th veterans, come early and find nearby parking. They lay claim to a Pinoy Hill prize: a picnic table under a large, leafy tree. Other families, later arrivals, must sit in the open on blankets in the early July sun. For my mom, being comfortable was important. She was starting to show.

On this day, the Hill is a bubble of frenetic activity and sound—outbursts of laughter and the steady hum of conversations in English, Bisayan, Ilocano, and at least one dialect I'd never heard before. The adults are glad for the respite from work and welcome the chance to renew friendships.

Kids my age are running around with abandon and playing games, which include baseball and badminton. Some are throwing firecrackers at each other. The rowdier boys are especially fond of firecrackers. One explodes right behind me, and I jump. Virginia turns, balls her fists, and scowls at my attacker, who scrambles away.

"Hey!" she yells. "You little shit." The boy doesn't stop or look back. She turns to me. "You okay?"

I nod. "Dang," I say. "Is it time to go fishin' yet?"

"Time to go."

"Dad knows?" I ask.

"Yes."

"Let's go."

Virginia starts slowly walking down the hill and turns back to make sure I am following. As the eldest, she always leads, and I always follow. Dad expects her to watch out for me, and I am grateful. She is my ever vigilant shadow, always aware, always on the job. With her I feel safe.

I love my sister, actually my half-sister. Her mom, Dad's first wife, is an Alaska Native. Mine is Filipino. After her mother died, she'd lived with Alex, her mom's Filipino boyfriend. Then, for whatever reason, she came to live with us. We have one father, two mothers. To me, the difference doesn't matter. It matters, though, to her.

We reach the lake, bait our hooks, and cast to a clear spot next to the lily pads.

"How's your piano lessons?" she asks.

"Okay," I say. "But I'd rather be playing baseball."

"You know, I asked Dad if I could take lessons," she says softly.

"What he say?"

"'Not now. We can't afford it.'"

The piano teacher is an old and tiny, elegantly dressed Black woman who loves Beethoven, Brahms, and Mozart. She sips tea with one hand, pinkie delicately extended, while wielding a pencil to bang my erring fingers with the other.

"Fortissimo!" she screeches as she pounds away. "This is not fortissimo. Not fortissimo at all. Didn't you practice?"

No, I say to myself, as I try to keep from crying. This past week I was fielding grounders and chasing flies. I love baseball, but I hate Beethoven. I hate classical music, and I hate you.

Most of her students are young Filipino kids, whose immigrant parents believe that playing the piano—like Liberace plays the piano—will open the door to packed concert halls, success, a house in the suburbs, and a better life than they will ever have. This is just one more myth in their new land.

Virginia, the author, Mom, and Dad, circa 1952. Photo courtesy of the author.

I'm not her pencil's only victim. Word of her finger pounding ways had become common knowledge. Black parents wise up, and their kids stop coming around.

"But my teacher, she's mean as an old rattlesnake," I say to Virginia.

"That's not the point."

At ten, I'm not sure what the point is.

But Virginia falls silent and focuses on her red-and-white bobber, which starts moving just a little. She slowly reaches down to pick up her pole and reels in some line.

"Shh," she says.

Suddenly, the bobber dips and skitters across the surface. Virginia calmly flicks her wrist back, setting the hook. A fat rainbow jumps out of the water, then makes a run. Virginia coolly reels in the slack, maintaining tension in the line. She continues reeling until she lands the fish, which is now flopping on the sand.

I'm giddy, beside myself. "A trout!" I shout. "Oh boy, look at that. A trout."

"You think your mom'll cook it?"

"Today? Nah."

"You're probably right," she says. "That's why I'm doing this." She bends over, removes the hook, and releases it into the water.

"But Virginia," I protest.

"It's always better fresh," she says. "I learned that from my mom." She looks at her watch. "It's almost four. I told Dad we'd be back by then. We better go."

I pout, and she stares at me.

"We better go," she repeats.

I shrug, and we gather our gear and begin walking. For most of the walk we are silent until we reach the crest of the hill. We stop.

"Dad's been different, more distant," she says.

"So?"

"I dunno, but I think something's up."

"Like what?"

"Alex came by last week," she says. "For no reason, out of the blue. He was in the kitchen talking to Dad and your mom. I didn't hear what they said." She paused. "But I'm worried."

Virginia and I resume walking and finally reach Dad and Mom's picnic table. They're packing up, getting ready to leave.

"Where's the fish?" Dad asks.

"Still in the lake," I say.

Dad laughs and tousles my hair. He glances at his daughter but doesn't say anything. She smiles. He doesn't smile back. Two weeks later, Virginia is gone.

✦

In my dream it is now seven years later, 1967. I am northwest of Seward Park on Empire Way South and inside the Filipino Community Center of Seattle. Since the building opened two years earlier, I had been there several times, attending dances, queen contests, and wedding receptions.

But today is Sunday, and the Filipino Community Council is meeting. One of the speakers, the father of one of my friends, stands and addresses the council.

"Negroes are leading the campaign for open housing in this city," he begins solemnly. "They deserve our support in a struggle that impacts us all."

In 1967 Seattle was a segregated city, with few Blacks, Filipinos, Jews, and other minorities living north of the Montlake Bridge or on Capitol Hill, Queen Anne Hill, and in other white neighborhoods. Many realtors and white homeowners simply refused to sell homes to buyers from these disfavored groups.

That included my family, which had considered moving out of the Central Area to a larger home in North Seattle. My parents inspected the property, and I was along for the ride. We liked what we saw. It was bigger than our tiny house on 32nd Avenue East. I was excited.

Dad made an offer. Later that day the realtor called. Dad had gone to Chinatown, so Mom answered the phone. She shared the receiver with me.

"The owners are now telling me they won't sell," the realtor said.

"Because we're Filipino?" Mom asked.

"I don't know."

Mom was angry, insistent. She'd lived long enough in America to know the answer. "Because we're Filipino," she said loudly, her voice more statement than question.

There was silence on the line.

"Yes," he finally said. "I'm sorry."

She slammed down the receiver.

At the time, this form of discrimination was common, reflecting the views of an overwhelmingly white, conservative town. It was also legal.

Just three years earlier, Seattle voters had rejected an open housing ordinance, which would have banned discrimination in housing. The campaign for fair housing continued, but it took the murder of Martin Luther King Jr., and the eruption of violence in scores of American cities, to give it the push it needed. The heat was on.

In April 1968, just three weeks after King's death, the Seattle City Council passed an open housing ordinance. For years, open housing had been the council's hottest political potato—thoroughly scrutinized, endlessly debated, inevitably tabled, and frequently kicked down the road. Yet supporters of the measure made sure it would not go away. It was clear that King's death had changed both the city and the nation. This was a hard, new reality not lost on city officials. The ordinance passed unanimously.

The Pinoys I knew were glad that it happened. To this day, I am as well. It was progress, but with a price. Being able to move also expanded the geographical boundaries of the Pinoy Seattle I knew. The old community was especially cohesive because of Filipino concentrations in the Central Area, Chinatown, and adjoining neighborhoods.

My friends' homes were within walking distance or just a short bus ride or drive away. We knew each other's backgrounds, we ate and drank at each other's kitchen tables. We knew the history and the traditions, the legends, attitudes, and beliefs of this community.

Then my family moved north in 1970. The Berganos and other Pinoy families moved as well. Filipinos were no longer confined to the Central Area, Chinatown, the South End, and Beacon Hill. It was harder to stay in touch.

A growing stream of newer immigrants, especially those with college degrees and professional training, spread themselves throughout the city and beyond. They were disconnected from the lived experiences and the physical landmarks that mattered to two earlier generations. For too many of the newcomers, the history of this community began when they arrived. They would set the standards; they would set the rules.

One evening, I was attending a wedding reception at the community center and found myself chatting with an electrical engineer. He hailed from Manila, newly arrived and working for Boeing.

"So," he said. "You are Filipino?"

"Yes," I replied.

"You are full-blooded?"

"Both sides," I answered. "Mom and Dad, they're from Cebu."

He nodded, seemingly in approval.

"Oh my goodness, you are so tall," he said, looking up. "Hmm, but even with your parents you are not a pure Filipino."

"What do you mean?"

"You don't speak Tagalog."

I looked at him, gritting my teeth and faking a smile, trying hard to keep my head from exploding. "No," I said calmly. "I speak Bisayan." I turned and walked away.

A "pure Filipino" litmus test, I thought. It was something new and one most of my Pinoy peers could never pass. Some had white or Native or Black parents. Only a few could speak Tagalog or any other Filipino language.

And what about our friends who ran with us but had no Filipino blood at all? They thought they were Pinoys. We did, too.

"Fuck you, you arrogant little prick," I muttered to myself.

In the 1970s, largely because of the new immigrants, the city's Filipino population grew substantially. Change is normal. But larger isn't always better, at least not to me. The old, once cohesive and sustaining sense of community that I knew began to weaken, shrivel, and shrink.

For young Pinoys this was a very special time, when we were able to define ourselves and create a sense of origin and belonging. That era is gone now, a relic of the distant past. Decades later, I miss it still.

WAS IT THAT LONG AGO?

THE SHIP ON TEMPLE STREET

Vince promised Reme an America he couldn't deliver.

Dad returned to Cebu in 1949 after more than twenty years in America, determined to find a wife. That's where he met my mom, Remedios Abella, a tall and lovely woman, who could have had her pick of eligible bachelors—successful young bankers, rich young lawyers, and the like.

In normal times, Dad wouldn't have had a chance. In America he was a migrant worker, older than Mom by seventeen years, and he hadn't gone beyond grade school.

But the postwar years in Cebu were not normal times. And unlike his competitors, Vince had an ace card to play. He was a US citizen, and the America of Filipino dreams would be their home.

She consented, and just days later they were married.

For Mom, the promise of America in 1949 must have been powerful. Cebu, and most of the Philippines, had been occupied by the Japanese during World War II. But guerrilla attacks continued, as did the terror unleashed by the Japanese military on civilians.

The island was liberated by American and Filipino forces in 1945, but the psychic and physical damage had been done. During the war, the occupation, and the resistance, friends and family had died, including two of Mom's brothers.

Her prewar home had become an island of nightmares, dark memories, and lingering sorrow. Mom left Cebu for the new land in 1949. She had no choice.

Dad had his own reasons for leaving America and traveling to Cebu. His marriage to an Alaska Native woman was floundering, still afloat but going slowly down the drain. And with it four kids, my older half-brothers and half-sisters, to whom he was indifferent.

At forty-two, he wanted to start over, and going to Cebu would give him that chance.

That's what Mom told me on a fall day a decade or so ago before dementia paid a visit and kidnapped her mind.

I remember the day, an overcast fall Sunday, mid-morning. We were sitting in the dining room of my sister's house, where Mom lived then, sipping tea. Irma had told me that she was starting to forget, starting to forget she'd forgotten, starting to repeat herself. There were good days and bad, Irma said.

As was my custom each week, I had driven up from Tacoma to spend time with her and just talk and sip tea or take her to mass. This Sunday was a good day.

Mom was in her eighties then, still cogent, but I knew time was not a friend. These precious Sunday visits would eventually become a slice of memory, a ritual of the past. She had answers to questions I still wanted to ask.

"So you get to Seattle . . ."

"And then I had you," she said. "Just right off the boat. Columbus Hospital, close to Saint James. It became Cabrini Hospital, you know. Named after the saint." She paused. "Is Cabrini still there?"

"No."

"Sayang, eh? I really liked that hospital. Special, you know? When you were born, the doctors and the nurses, they were so nice." She frowned. "What happened?" She paused, still frowning. "Something did. What did I miss?" she asked.

"Just changes in this city, Mom. Progress. New construction, renovation, that sorta thing. It's not the small town that we knew."

She turned to look out the window. "You know, I wish I would have seen it one more time, just to feel and remember," she said softly.

"I know," I said, and glanced at my watch. Almost 11 a.m. I'd promised a pal I'd meet him in Chinatown for roast pork, Chinese greens, and rice. I knew this story. She'd told it to me before. I had to nudge her back on track.

"Ah, Mom," I began. "What did you and Dad do next?"

"Well, we brought you home, and Dad went out looking for work," she said. "Your father, he was always looking for work. But after a few weeks, no luck."

"And then?"

"And then he said let's go to Los Angeles. His townmate told him there's work there. So we packed what we had, got in the car, and drove."

I looked at my mother. "Los Angeles?" My eyes widened. I hadn't heard this story before. "I didn't know we were there."

"Yes, we were," she confirmed. "Just after you were born. We were there for more than a year."

"Where'd we stay?"

"Temple Street. Lots of Pinoys, most were old-timers like your dad," she said slowly. "We lived in a small apartment. Run-down, yes, the entire block was run-down, like skid row. But it was all Dad could afford." Mom shook her head. "Those times, Peter. Those times were very hard."

I took a deep breath.

"When he was at work, I'd take care of you," she began. "And after you were asleep and I was done cooking and trying to clean, I would lie on the bed and cry. Just cry. Good for me you slept so well. We were so poor, wondering where the next job, the next meal was coming from."

She put her right palm, slender fingers extended, to the side of her cheek and slowly shook her head. "Would we be living on the street?"

Her eyes twitched. For a moment the trace of a grimace, a memory of despair. Then she composed herself, the grimace now gone.

"And then come to find out he's got a wife and Virginia and all these other kids," she finally said. "Oh my gosh, *ay-yay-yay-yay*, he never said a thing about them when he courted me in Cebu." Mom rolled her eyes and sighed. "Messy, so messy. And I, uh, sometimes it was just too much."

"So, um, why didn't you leave?"

Mom looked at me like she couldn't believe the question. "And go where?"

I had no answer.

"Anyway," she continued. "Dad found a new job, more hours, more pay, and things weren't so tight. And on Sunday, your father and I would dress up for mass, then go to the Chinese café on the corner. We'd sit down and order chop suey and almond chicken."

Mom paused. "You'd sit in your high chair, and I'd give you a small piece of chicken, and you'd eat it with your hands. And you'd laugh, and gurgle, play with chicken and put it in your mouth. The chicken was so good, and I remember thinking to myself, 'This boy, my firstborn child, he's a happy one.'"

I smiled, trying to imagine the scene. "I don't remember," I said.

"Of course not. You were one."

"So then what happened?"

"I started to make friends."

Mom explained that some of the old Pinoys had returned to the Philippines to find younger wives. Some had served in the First Filipino Regiment, part of the American force that liberated the Philippines. After the war, others, like my dad, had gone back on their own. A few of the newlyweds had settled on Temple Street.

"One was this young girl from Cebu, a new arrival, couldn't have been more than twenty," Mom said. "Even now I can see her face, but I don't remember her name. Ooh, her name, her name, wowee, it's been so long." Mom closed then opened her eyes. "Inday, let's just call her Inday," she said, using the fallback name for any nameless female.

I smiled. "Inday works."

"Well, I met her at the café," Mom said, "where she was working as a waitress, part-time, and Inday walks by our table and Dad and I, we're talking, and she overhears. Then she stops and introduces herself in Bisayan. And before you know it, she's visiting our place, and I'm visiting hers. Each day, or at least most days when she wasn't working." Mom sighed. "Inday, she was so young, so innocent."

"What do you mean?"

"Well, we were at our apartment sitting in the kitchen," Mom said. "And it was a hot day, August I think. I'd opened all the windows, and we were sitting at the kitchen table drinking soda pop with ice, just talking about the usual things."

"Like what?"

"Oh, you know," she said with a wave of her hand. "How we were doing, how we were adjusting. How lonely it was here. How we missed our families. How we missed home, especially how we missed home. Just the usual things when we got together."

"And then?"

Mom smiled. "And then all of a sudden our junky old refrigerator acts up and starts to make these loud noises, like a roar, or a growl, or a car engine firing up. And Inday, she's startled and stands up and makes the sign of the cross. And I tell her to relax."

"So, what else did you tell her?"

"Well, I look at her and reach to hold her hand and say, sit, sit, please sit, don't be worried, and I explained to her slowly, that what she just heard . . . was the sound . . . of the engine . . . of the ship . . . that will take me home." Mom chuckled. "And do you know what she says next?"

I smiled, sensing a punch line. "No, Mom, of course not."

"Hoy, Reme," she said. "How did they get a ship all the way to Temple Street?"

I laughed. Mom did, too.

It was time to leave. I stood and walked over to kiss her on the forehead. "Gotta go," I said. "But I'll be back, same time next week."

"Drive careful."

"Of course."

As I walked to the door, Mom was laughing again. I was, too.

"Ah, new immigrants," I heard her say. "Bless their hearts. They're so easy to fool."

BAD ATTITUDE

I f there was an American phrase beloved by my dad and his generation and passed along to their American-born sons, it's this: Fuck you.

It's what they said to white men on a racist and violent West Coast when Pinoys wore zoot suits, hung out on street corners, and dated (and often married) white women.

"Monkeys" you called us. "Monkeys go home," you screamed.

Fair enough, then we will use our secret jungle potions and our "jungle boogie" dancing to lure your women and not give them back. White men, we will break your laws against race mixing. We will mongrelize your tribe, and as you get older, we will live in your cities and towns, maybe even your neighborhoods. You will watch our children grow and have the better lives that we could never have. May you shrivel in your hatred. May you die unmourned, unloved.

Fuck you.

That's also what the manongs said in the 1930s when they formed militant labor unions, striking and sometimes wildcat striking their way to better wages and conditions in the fields and salmon canneries.

Finally, it's what the legendary labor leader Larry Itliong told farmers in Delano when he led Filipino grape pickers off the fields in 1965. The ongoing strike caught the nation's attention and led to the pop culture beatification of the humble, pious, and made-for-television Cesar Chavez, who led the Mexican workers.

In too many narratives Filipinos played a marginal role or were ignored altogether. But make no mistake: It was the younger, less certain, and less experienced Chavez who followed Itliong off the fields, not the other way around. This defiance was inherited by their American-born sons.

Flash forward to what a Pinoy buddy said about the US Army when he got his draft notice during the Vietnam War. "Fuck the army," he said defiantly. "I'm joinin' the Marines." To me, the first part made sense, the second, maybe not so much. But I understood the attitude.

Misguided? Maybe. But defiant—like father like son, very Pinoy.

It's also what another friend, Eddie, said a second before he punched an off-duty cop in the head. I shouldn't have even been at the scene in that junior high gym on a week-day night. I was in law school prepping for the next day's class when my buddy Steve called.

"Grab your tennis shoes," he said. "Rec league game, and the Pinoys are a couple dudes short. Be by in ten."

Why not? I needed a break from wills and trusts.

The Filipino team was a motley crew with a changing cast of characters who smoked cigarettes and never practiced between games. T-shirts, shorts, cutoffs, and sweatpants were our uniform for the night.

My playing days, years in the past, allowed me to take a spot on the bench, catch up with friends, and watch the game, a mismatch from the start. The Filipinos were much shorter and thinner than our beefier and taller opponents. But the differences didn't end there.

The cops actually called out and ran plays, set screens, and looked for the open man. They played defense, wore matching uniforms, and practiced during the week. In contrast, Pinoy ballers were not inclined to pass or to pay attention to the other basic aspects of teamwork. On offense, dribble and shoot was how we played, which meant that the first one to touch the ball was also the last, which was cool because we understood it.

Our style of play was less about winning, although sometimes that happened, and more about highlighting individual skills and drawing *oohs* and *aahs* from appreciative teammates and fans for the distance-defying jump shot. Or better still, a quick drive to the hole, avoiding flailing defenders too slow to respond.

In other words, art versus function on this junior high school basketball court. And tonight, art was getting stomped. Down by ten after five minutes, I knew it would only get worse. I leaned back in my chair and turned to Rey, a friend I hadn't seen in months.

"Hey, man," I began but didn't finish the sentence.

"Motherfucker, fuck you!" a familiar voice from the court screamed, followed by a loud *thwack*.

"Ah, man," Rey said. "It's Eddie."

Eddie's victim, bent over and moaning, held a hand over his eye. His brother cops formed a protective circle around him. *Like yaks,* I thought, but smaller, whiter, and not as furry.

One teammate handed the wounded cop a towel to stop the bleeding from a cut above the eye. Another walked him off the court.

"Your boy hit me in the balls!" Eddie screamed, glaring and pointing angrily at the cops. "What the hell would you do?"

At 5'10", 170 pounds, Eddie wasn't physically imposing. Other dangerous men were bigger and stronger, but no one was as fierce. He was a berserker and would gladly fight anyone dumb enough to step forward to take him on.

No one did.

As the impasse continued, Rey sighed, then stood up and walked onto the court. "Come on, brotha' may need some backup." The rest of us joined him.

As it turned out, Eddie didn't need our help. The cops turned and walked toward their bench, picked up their bags, and left.

"Fuck this!" one screamed as he walked out the door. "You're just lucky we're cops."

We were lucky? Sure, I thought, an embarrassing off-duty brawl and its consequences—bad publicity, letters of reprimand, maybe even suspensions without pay. Consequences considered, no doubt.

But also considered was snarling, dangerous Eddie, a foaming two-legged dog willing to fight any one or all of them, one-on-one or all at once.

Almost fifty years later, my bottom line: The cops were lucky, too.

✦

I sit here remembering, knowing that the first generation has vanished and that their children have had children, perhaps grandchildren, too. And that these stories, their stories, although they have much in common with the stories of other immigrants from Asia, the manongs' attitude of defiance is unique. Such stories have not been told, or if told, have been forgotten or not listened to by too many younger Filipinos.

But that indifference may be slowly changing. Young Filipinos have gone to Delano, visiting, writing about, and producing films focused on Larry Itliong and the pivotal Filipino role in the 1965 Delano grape strike. In terms of shining, defiant moments in Pinoy history, it is hard to top Itliong and the Delano Pinoys for what they did in 1965.

But such a moment does exist. In Seattle its all-but-forgotten details described in a lawsuit argued before the US Supreme Court, *ILWU Local 37 v. Boyd* (1954).

Every spring, Local 37 sent thousands of Pinoys north to the Alaska salmon canneries. But the United States was in the middle of the Communist-hunting tsunami unleashed by Senator Joseph McCarthy, and Boyd, the Seattle-based district director of Immigration and Naturalization Services (INS), was more than happy to do his part.

His target: Local 37.

In 1953 Boyd's office twisted federal immigration law and threatened "to treat aliens domiciled in the continental United States returning from temporary work in Alaska as if they were aliens entering the United States for the first time." By 1953 many of Local 37's members had become American citizens, against whom Boyd's threat would not apply. But others were not.

When the Philippines became independent in 1946, it cut the legal tie between America and its former colony. It also changed the status of thousands of Pinoys. Overnight, and despite decades in America, they lost their status (and protection) as American nationals.

Aliens are what they became. And under US law, aliens seeking entry to this country for the first time could be excluded for any number of reasons, including disfavored political affiliations.

Chris Mensalvas, the local's president, was the unreachable itch that triggered Boyd's obsession. Among Filipinos, the one-legged Mensalvas was legendary—committed, courageous, and tough—and Pinoys, no strangers to hardship, admired these traits.

But he was also an unabashed Communist, unforgivable during the paranoia of the McCarthy era, when many Americans yearned for peace and for simple answers to the questions raised by an increasingly complex and hostile postwar world. In 1945 the US and its allies had defeated fascism. Yet just the next year, Winston Churchill warned of an "iron curtain" caused by the Soviet Union's aggressive westward expansion. Then, in 1949, China—an important wartime ally—fell to Communist forces in that country's civil war. And finally, in 1950, American soldiers were battling Chinese Communists on the Korean Peninsula.

The speed and sheer scope of the global changes were breathtaking—and not at all to America's liking. Within this unsettling milieu, Senator Joe McCarthy provided the snake oil to soothe the nation's jangled nerves. Subversives, he claimed, were the problem, and he knew who they were: Communists and sympathizers could be found in government, universities, labor unions, and the arts. His charges, most of which were unfounded, were dutifully reported by a meek and uncritical American press. But in the early 1950s the McCarthy era had shaped the tenor of American life, giving rise to blacklists, arrests, guilt by innuendo and association, terminations, and ruined lives.

In those days the INS building and Local 37's headquarters were within walking distance of each other. It must have galled Boyd and other immigration officials that a Communist-led union could be so brazen as to openly operate and thrive in the agency's backyard.

Hence the threat in 1953.

INS's goal, I am sure, was to force the rank-and-file to remove Mensalvas. But he continued as president until 1959, or five years after McCarthy was censured by the Senate and two years after McCarthy's death in 1957.

And each spring and despite the threat, Local 37 would send Pinoys north for decades to come.

But why were these workers, most of whom were not Communists, so unfailingly loyal to a marked man? For starters, group solidarity strengthened by years of racial hostility had become an article of faith shared by members of the first Pinoy generation.

This is how we survived.

But that's not all. In 1984 I wrote this about Mensalvas:

They stayed loyal to Chris because he understood them and their needs, and he spoke their language. That was his magic. He could speak to anyone, and that person would believe, or would at least want to believe . . . Chris's talent—that human touch—worked in spite of his ideology, not because of it.

In retrospect, the rank-and-file's defiance was both brave and audacious during a time when other Americans drew their shades and cowered in their homes, and turncoats kept busy naming names. But not at Local 37, where union members made abundantly clear that they, not the federal government, would choose who they wanted to lead them.

That's our decision. It's who we are, the old Pinoys said.

And oh, one more thing, Mr. Boyd, Mr. Big Shot, Mr. Polished Florsheim Shoes: Fuck you.

GABRIEL

Despite his years, Gabriel keeps clunking along, leaving
Seattle, heading east as the sun rises, destination Walla
Walla. Inside the twelve-year-old Plymouth are a husband
and wife, their son, almost four, and an infant, his brother.
It's May 1954, harvest season, and the husband's going to
run an asparagus crew.

Migrant work is a tough, backbreaking life; stay too long
and it will bend your back and gnarl your fingers. But it's the
only life he's ever known for over thirty years, since he came
from the Philippines to America those distant decades ago.

They reach Walla Walla at sunset. The husband and wife
grab the bags and walk to their quarters—a rundown wooden
shack on the edge of the fields. The thin walls are no barrier
to the heat. Inside, the air is dusty and hot, unbearably so.

The baby, lying on a bed, starts to cry. She wipes his face
with a cold, wet wash towel. The crying stops. She faces her

*husband and speaks in a loud whispered Bisayan. Her slen-
der body shudders with every word. Her arms flail, and her
fists clench and unclench, clench and unclench. She points
to the baby. She points to me.*

*The husband turns away and tilts his head back, as if
to calm himself and gather his thoughts. He takes a deep
breath, then turns to face her.*

*She is sobbing now, bent over, hands covering her face.
He draws her to him.*

Their son watches.

The next day they are gone.

Another Sunday morning and I'm visiting with my
mother more than a decade after Dad died and about
a year before all of those years start kidnapping her
mind. This morning, though, she is chipper, sharp, happy,
still outside the endless loop of Philippine childhood memories. We're sitting at the kitchen table, chatting about
everything and nothing at all. A typical Sunday morning
with Mom.

"Do you remember Walla Walla?" I ask.

She looks surprised. "Ay yay yay, so, you remember
that?"

"Yeah, some of it, but it's been so long ago."

She sighs. "When I was younger, I could have married
anyone in Cebu. A young attorney from the best mestizo
family, the Chinese owner of the biggest bank, anyone.
They all courted me." Mom looks away and smiles, possibly
at the thought of having once been a beauty.

I nod. I had seen the old sepia pictures. Mom in her
twenties—tall, elegant, beautiful.

"And then one day your father comes around. He's good looking, yes, and a US citizen, but he's older and not as handsome as the others. Still . . ." Mom drums the table with her fingertips.

"You know, I still miss him," she says softly. "It hurts, but less so now. Progress, no?"

I nod. "So why . . ."

"There was something about him," she says. "Something fierce and confident. And then he puffs out his chest—you know how he used to do it—and he tells me, 'Hoy, I'm a big man in the States, a boss, a big shot; you will never have to worry.' And that was it."

She pauses.

"We married a week later."

She laughs.

"And after we came here and you were born, that's all I did."

"Huh?"

"Worry. About food, where we were going to stay, how would we survive. Everything. You're too young to remember, but we were living in a junk apartment in Los Angeles. Your father wasn't what he said he was. Dad was looking for work, anything. He would find a job, then get laid off. Find a job, then get laid off again." She looked away, her brow furrowed, her eyes squinting, as if the next sentence—here just a second ago—had so artfully dodged beyond her reach.

"Oh yes," she finally said. "So, ah, where was I? Oh yes, we drive back to Seattle. Dad worked more here, low pay, but it was longer term, better than nothing."

She gazed out the window.

"And then Walla Walla."

"Did you regret your choice?"

Mom stares at me. "What do you mean?"

"Marrying him."

"At the start yes," she says slowly, unsure if this is a secret to be told. "But over time, no. We changed, he changed, and your father's the one I've loved the most."

"So what did you tell him in Walla Walla?"

"I tell him, 'Hoy, listen to me. This is no life for children, and if we don't leave tomorrow, I'm taking the kids and going home.'"

"To Seattle?" he asks.

"Cebu," I say, "Mr. Big Shot, Mr. Big Talk Fancy Pants. And you will never see me or them again." She stops, as if reliving the scene—relishing its colors, its heat, her emotions.

"Mom," I say. "Would you have left?"

"Yes," she quietly says.

Mystery solved. So that's how Mom ended the only way of life Dad had ever known. My father was stubborn beyond reason, not prone to changing his mind. A hard, bitter life had taught him that. For him, a changed mind was a sign of weakness.

But this time he did. And we prospered because of it. From then on, he stayed put, eventually landing a welding job at Kenworth Motors, where he worked for twenty years.

I then edited my memory, adding audio to my Walla Walla video, inserting Mom's voice and words into the scene. "And you will never see me or them again"—an ending Dad would have died to avoid.

I was silent for a moment, counting my blessings, among them having this woman before me as my mother.

"Thanks, Mom," I say as I rise to leave. "But I'd better hit the road. Don't want to catch the freeway traffic, know what I mean?" I walk over to kiss her. "I-5 can be such a bitch."

As I turn toward the door, Mom says, "Don't go yet. Can you take me . . ."

I turn around.

"Take me to the cemetery. I'm missing him," she says. "He would like to see us both. I've got this feeling . . ."

I shrug and retrace my steps. "I'm sure he would."

NOT QUITE CAMELOT

For many of my generation, the early 1960s was a time of hope and giddy optimism, with the start of a new decade, the charismatic John Fitzgerald Kennedy and his elegant wife Jacqueline, with this nation's best and the brightest now in charge. As a young boy, I stayed up with my folks to watch the presidential election, closing my eyes and praying hard for JFK to win.

And when he did, I could feel the magic: Camelot redux. The Kennedys were Catholic; I was, too. We were now related, or at least members of the same sprawling tribe.

For me, it was a great time to be a kid in America. It was a great time to be a Catholic. What could possibly go wrong?

A lot, as it turned out.

In 1961 Kennedy gave the green light to a CIA-sponsored invasion of Cuba to topple its Communist leader Fidel Castro. In a classic case of big power arrogance and wishful thinking, the United States assumed that Castro and the revolution he led were not supported by the Cuban people—but they were wrong. The invaders, more than fourteen hundred Cuban expatriates, were quickly killed or captured.

For the United States, the invasion—popularly known as the Bay of Pigs—was a fiasco, an abysmal Cold War failure. And worse, it strengthened the ties between Cuba and the Soviet Union and helped set the stage for what happened next.

October 1962 brought America and the world the Cuban Missile Crisis, when the Soviets had snuck nuclear missiles into Cuba and the United States in response mounted a naval blockade and demanded that the weapons be withdrawn. For thirteen days both nations danced on the narrow ledge of nuclear annihilation until the Soviets blinked and the crisis ended.

In the documentary *The Fog of War,* Robert McNamara, secretary of defense at the time, stares at the camera and says, "At the end we lucked out." He extends his left index finger and thumb, which are almost touching. "We came that close," McNamara says, to a nuclear shootout—and the end of the world.

I saw the film years ago when it first came out. And I recently saw it again. The impact was the same: McNamara's words still gave me chills.

Of course, at twelve I wasn't sitting at the Cabinet meetings. I didn't know just how close we were to disaster. But even then, I knew I was suddenly living in a far more dangerous world. I had seen newsclips and black-and-white photos of billowing mushroom clouds and the devastation of Hiroshima and Nagasaki and was horrified by what I saw: the wide-eyed stares of survivors, the open sores of children and their peeling skin.

My young boy conclusion: The lucky ones were those who died immediately.

Even now, those October days and the fear I felt are seared in my memory. During the week I would go to school, pretend to pay attention, joke with my friends, and shoot hoops after class. Later, I would hang out with my friend George at Frank's, the local drug store. There we loaded up on Hershey bars, potato chips, and Cokes, then went outside and talked about baseball, our favorite sport. It was our young kid ritual. It's what we always did.

"The Giants, man, next year they gonna take it all," George declared as he chomped down on a Hershey. "Man, they got Willie," he said, in between bites.

"And don't forget McCovey and Marichial," I added with a nod. "Phew, dang, they sure be loaded, that's for sure."

"They sure are," he said. He looked away for a moment, then gathered himself and asked, "Hey man, you scared?"

"Of what?"

"You know . . ."

"Nah," I said breezily, then stopped. What was the point? George knew me as well as anyone. I took a deep breath. "I, uh, uh, yeah, I guess I am."

"Me, too," he said.

I walked home, watched Walter Cronkite on the evening news, and ate dinner. On the surface it all seemed so normal—a Monday through Friday school-day routine, but it wasn't.

"Will we be alive tomorrow?" I asked Mom.

She sighed. "Just say your prayers," she said, as she glanced at the clock. "It's late, son. Time to sleep."

In my room I folded my hands, knelt by my bed, and closed my eyes. "Please don't let us die," I whispered. This was my prayer for every one of those thirteen nerve-racking days.

✦

More than fifty years later, they were suddenly back, those gnawing and unwelcome long-ago fears. With growing apprehension, I felt the need to repeat that prayer in 2017, when the untested Donald Trump and North Korea's Kim Jong Un recklessly traded insults, and tensions between the two nuclear armed nations built.

At one point, the former reality show host warned North Korea of "fire and fury like the world has never seen"—as if the world, after the mind-numbing horrors of Hiroshima and Nagasaki, had not seen enough.

I knew that if a shooting war started, China, North Korea's neighbor and powerful nuclear ally, would probably get involved. And then . . .

My belly knotted up. At the time I was teaching an evening class at The Evergreen State College in Tacoma. We were close to wrapping up. I scanned the room, looking at each of my students, almost all of them new, all of them older adults who'd added four hours to their workday to spend time with strangers.

Why? What were their goals, their dreams? Would they live long enough to achieve them? Was college their last chance to rewrite the script? Would we even survive this week?

In the time that remained, I was trying to remember their faces. I was trying to imagine their lives.

"Professor, when is the book review due?" a slender woman with salt-and-pepper hair asked. She was smiling, attentive, and seemed happy to be here.

"In class, next Tuesday," I said, as if I believed one more Tuesday was guaranteed. At that point, I just wasn't sure. I gathered my books and dismissed the class.

"If we're still here," I added.

✦

Camelot ended on November 22, 1963, when Father Marsh, our new young parish priest, made a surprise visit to our eighth-grade class at Saint Teresa.

This is odd, I thought. What brings him here? Christmas break is weeks away. It's too soon to hand us our report cards.

I glanced at the clock, 11:55, just minutes before lunch and recess and softball or soccer, my favorite part of the school day. I liked Father Marsh, but whatever he had to tell us, I was hoping it wouldn't last too long.

He stood at the front of the class, his arms extending downward, his hands folded in front of his cassock. He bowed his head and took a deep breath. "The President has been shot," he said quietly.

At first we were stunned, unbelieving, silent.

"The President has been shot," he repeated.

All fidgeting stopped. I sat stiff and still at my desk—the message processed then fully absorbed. I stared blankly at the blackboard and remember hearing the girl sitting behind me start to sniffle, then cry.

"We must pray for him," he said solemnly.

And so we prayed and cried—in the classroom and later, in church. Then we cried and prayed at home. But despite our fervent prayers, despite the volume of our tears, those five words could never be erased, taken back, edited. Or ever forgotten.

"The President has been shot," Father Marsh said on Friday, 11:55, November 22, 1963.

THE FISHING MAN

As a young boy I loved to read—from books and newspapers to magazines. Especially magazines. And especially *Field & Stream*, with its glossy pages on which my eleven-year-old eyes could *ahh* and *ooh* at photos of red-striped, tail-walking trout in their distant and pure mountain creek homes.

Next came the stories of the intrepid fly-fishing white men who caught (and sometimes released) them. Nature as it should be.

Such noble and beautiful fish, I thought at the time. Such noble and handsome men, none of whom I was sure called Seattle's Central Area, Chinatown, or South End home. I wanted to join their ranks. But first, I had to research how to become one of *them*.

I grabbed the dog-eared Sears catalog on the coffee table in our living room, skipping past (for the first time) women's summer beach wear and going straight to the sports section, the realm of the regal Ted Williams.

And there he was, Boston's Teddy Baseball himself, fly-fishing pole in hand, looking straight at the camera, looking straight at me. Ted winked and smiled.

"Ah, um, Mr. Williams," I stammered.

"Forget it, kid," he said. "I don't care how many paper routes you have or how much your allowance is. This pole, just by itself, look at the price, for chrissake. You can't afford this. Nope, no way. And then there's the travel. It costs a lot of money to get to Montana, or Idaho, or Wyoming where the pretty fish live. No way."

I nodded.

The great Williams stared at me, fondly, like maybe he was worried that speaking an obvious truth had hurt my feelings, or like maybe this conversation mattered.

He smiled. "Hey, kid, how old are you anyway?"

"Eleven, but I'll be twelve in a couple a—"

Ted chuckled, cutting me off. "Hey, don't feel bad. When I was your age, I couldn't afford this either. My mom, she's Mexican. Betcha didn't know that." Ted frowned and shook his head. "You know, back in my day, bein' Mexican in San Diego wasn't easy. But I lucked out. There was baseball, of course, and I was better than anyone else. But 'Williams,' hey, just like any Anglo name, right? So I had it a little easier. Now what about you, kid. You're what?"

"Filipino."

"Hmm, I thought so. Plenty of those where I come from. Hardworking, friendly, nose in the dirt, sweatin' out in the fields every damn summer day, just like Mexicans. And just like Mexicans, they're born poor, they die poor. Hell, none of 'em are rich. Least not the ones I knew."

Ted closed his eyes. Again, he shook his head. "I was lucky, kid," he said softly. "Baseball, my last name. Got to avoid much of that." He took a deep breath before refocusing on me. "You love baseball?"

"Yes, sir."

"You love fishing?"

"Yes, sir."

"What do you use?"

"A hand line," I replied. "My dad and me, on Sundays after mass we go to the docks west of downtown on Elliott Bay and jig for shiners, sometimes we get lucky and catch a perch. It's fun. Dad says he did this a lot during the Depression. Then sometimes on Saturday if we ain't playin' ball or somethin', me and my pals, a bunch of us, we just hop the 2 Madrona, get off downtown, walk to the dock, and do the same thing."

Ted nodded, approving. "Well, it's not stream fishing for browns in Montana, that's for sure. But it's a start. A lot of poor boys get started that way," he said. "But what you need now is a pole, just not a fly pole. And you can get one cheap. Or at least cheaper. Then all you gotta do is toss the bait from shore where the bigger fish are and just sit back and wait."

"Thanks, Mr. Williams," I said before closing the catalog. I turned and walked out of the room.

"Any time, kid," I heard him say.

I needed a pole, Mr. Williams told me. How to get one, now that was another issue. I knew that the basic fishing pole/spinning reel combos at Chubby & Tubby out on Rainier ran about twenty dollars. Not expensive, much less than fly-fishing gear, but at that moment twenty bucks was twenty more than I had.

It was a sunny late April afternoon, so I walked outside and sat on the front steps. My mind was focused, buried in thought as I raced past a list of money-generating choices.

Weekly allowance? Not enough.

Borrow money from friends? Broke like me.

Lawn mowing for neighbors? Allergic to grass. More allergic to manual labor.

What, then?

The answer came the next afternoon, Saturday, when my favorite uncle, Kikoy, dropped by the house. Quirico Daan, my dad's cousin, lived in a shabby Chinatown hotel, a cramped one-room, hot plate walk-up. As kids, Dad and he had come to this new land together, full of hope. But in the decades since, they'd lived their lives in America's dark margins—in West Coast fields and in Alaska's canneries, working dead-end, backbreaking jobs.

But unlike Dad, Kikoy had never married. He didn't have much money—as a cannery worker, that was a given, and even I knew that—but what he did earn he spent on nice clothes, nice whores, and me.

Over the years he treated me as his chosen son, not just a nephew. When I was young, Uncle Kikoy was my benefactor and my babysitter. He taught me how to curse. When he babysat me, he'd get dressed up, complete with crisp dress shirt and Borsalino hat, and we would prowl his favorite Chinatown haunts full of other old Pinoys. Like Kikoy, they were all nattily dressed, serenely confident, and speaking different languages—their words sounding like notes.

They were glad to be together. They were glad to be alive. And why not? Many, like Kikoy, were combat veterans. All of them had survived hard lives and racial hatred. Yet here they were, decades later, still joking and laughing and living in a land that didn't want them. On me these old Filipinos left an impression: That's what I wanna be when I grow up.

From those Pinoys, I first heard *cocksucker, sonamabitch, motherfucker*. They were among Kikoy's favorites, his friends' too, and were usually bellowed at the pool hall or at a card table in the Victory Bath House on King.

Uncle Kikoy was also my beloved giver of gifts and surprises. And, lucky me, today was no exception.

Dad and Kikoy were sitting at the kitchen table, chatting and laughing, eating apple pie and drinking coffee, with lotsa cream and sugar. As usual, I was camped nearby in the living room in front of our tiny black-and-white watching a show with a white boy and his horse or maybe a collie, I forget which.

"Hoy, boy," Dad commanded. "Come here."

I rose and walked toward them.

"Your uncle, he did well at the track."

Kikoy smiled and nodded. "Really good," he said as he rubbed his hands together. "Hit the trifecta. First time, all my years goin'. Boy oh boy."

"He wanna give you something," Dad said.

Uncle Kikoy reached under the table and handed me a new two-piece fiberglass rod complete with spin-cast reel with a covered front and its snazzy, newfangled push-button release. I recognized it, too—a Zebco combination that I'd first seen in the fishing gear aisle at Chubby & Tubby.

It caught my eye. *A black beauty*, I thought. But more than my folks could afford. And just like that, now it was mine. My jaw dropped. "Oh wow," I mumbled.

Dad looked at me sternly. "Boy, you got something else to say?"

"Thank you, Uncle Kikoy. Ah, um, thank you."

Kikoy giggled, then extended his right hand palm up and shook it, his wordless way of saying, It was nothin', kid, nothin'.

But to me, it was not nothing. From that day on, if I had free time and wasn't playing baseball or going to school, I was on my bike, the priceless Zebco dismantled and tethered to the crossbar, pedaling hard to some secret or not-so-secret spot on the Seattle side of Lake Washington.

In those days, the lake was polluted, the destination of untreated human waste. But being a kid, I just didn't care. *It didn't look polluted*, especially on clear early mornings when the lake glistened with the snow-capped Cascades in the background.

Health concerns settled, off on my bike I'd go on more days than not. From our little house in the Central Area, it's about three miles to Lake Washington—for me and my young legs, an easy stretch by any measure. But it may as well have been three hundred. Across the street from the lake were the mansions and fancy houses of Seattle's best—the ghost people—the white movers and shakers who ran the city. They were rarely seen, at least not by folks in the Central Area.

But I wasn't curious about them at all—their great houses and great wealth, their large lives and grand dreams, their glittering futures or heroic past. All I knew was that rich folks didn't own the lake, and they didn't own the view.

In my grade school years of fishing the lake—before I was consumed by high school sports—my favorite spot was the dock next to Madison Beach. For me, it wasn't the most productive, but that's where I met the Fishing Man, a stocky and older African American. Every time I went to that spot, he was there, sitting on a folding chair—bending forward if it was cold, leaning back if it wasn't.

He wasn't a man of many words, so intent was he on catching fish. But over time we sometimes chatted. One afternoon he told me he was born in Louisiana, came up during the war, served in the Pacific, and returned to Seattle, settling here. Before he retired, he'd worked the shipyards. Then his wife died, and his kids grew up and moved away.

"Why Seattle?" I asked.

He looked at me. "Louisiana," he answered. "Hard place to be if you colored."

One day, late afternoon, I arrived at the dock. The Fishing Man had already caught a messa perch, many more than usual. I watched him reel in his line and rebait the hook—worm and salmon eggs, staples. Then he added a small marshmallow.

"Perch eat marshmallows?"

"These ones do," he replied. He stood and cast as far as he could, then settled into his chair. "Eat this, bitches," I heard him mumble.

✦

Almost sixty years later, I am sitting on a dock on American Lake near my home outside Tacoma. I carefully bait the hook—worm, salmon egg, and marshmallow, a food combination not normally found in nature. But it works, and for me, that's the bottom line.

I cast out and hear the plunk and watch the ripple. I tighten the line. This morning in early May is warm, so I sit back and relax. And then a fleeting memory, a glimpse: *Field & Stream* and the white fly-fishing men.

Nope, I never became one of them.

Then I take out a Camel. I light it, welcome the first drag, and smile. My eyes focus on the tip of the pole.

"Eat this, bitches," I say.

THE CURVE

A curve ball ended my baseball playing days.

It was tough, too, because baseball was my first love. I looked forward to the annual ritual of going to Chubby & Tubby and picking out my cheap Japanese glove and one cheap rubber hardball, which, unlike its more expensive leather-covered cousin, wouldn't come apart when it hit an asphalt surface.

When I got home, I would oil it down, put the ball in the mitt, wrap it in tape, put it under my pillow, and sleep on it. In the morning, the glove would be soft and flexible, ready to go.

I loved baseball because it started in the spring, my favorite season. But I also loved it because it had the Brooklyn Dodgers, my favorite sports team of all time. This was the Dodgers of the great Jackie Robinson and Pee Wee Reese and Gil Hodges and Roy Campanella, an elite and integrated team working and winning together, decades ahead of America. For me, the story of the pre–Los Angeles Dodgers in the 1950s filled me with hope, allowing me to imagine my country as it could be, not as it was.

I had never actually seen the Brooklyn Dodgers play, but I had read about them. Mom bought me a book on baseball history, and I devoured it, especially the chapter on the Dodgers and their Captain Ahab's quest for a World Series championship. I learned that over the decades the Dodgers were frequent visitors to the Series, and each time they'd been turned away, often by the New York Yankees.

As a kid, I grew to hate the Yankees—so regal, arrogant, and successful, so Mickey Mantle and Whitey Ford, so white. Then I read that the Dodgers finally won the title, in 1955, and I relaxed and exhaled. Here, finally, was justice and a better world, at least for a year.

My good friend George also loved baseball. As kids, we'd play the game, then dream about what we'd become.

"A Dodger," I solemnly declared one hot two-Coke July afternoon. We were sitting under a tree near the diamond at Garfield High, waiting for practice to start.

"Imma play second base just like Jackie. I wanna wear his number, too."

George paused and looked at me, thoughtfully. "Man, you gotta fly in airplanes, you know, to get to games 'n shit," he said. "And I know you hate flying. You told me so yourself."

"Hmm," I said. "Hadn't thought about that."

During spring and summer, George and I would spend hours reading baseball magazines and trading baseball cards, arguing over the merits of great Black and Latin stars, players with whom we could identify and even some who looked like us.

"Willie Mays," George would declare. "Dude's got power, and he also got style. Um, that basket catch. Showin' off, like it ain't no big thing. Easy as pie. Man, now that's style. Ain't no one like him. Willie's the best. No doubt about it."

"Not so fast," I would counter. "Roberto Clemente, such quick wrists, so smooth and fast, runs the bases and covers right field, like a deer, I tell ya, just like a deer."

And then there was Bobby Balcena, the Filipino Flyer, who played center field for the Seattle Rainiers at Sicks Stadium. Bobby was good and even went up to the Bigs for what baseball guys call a "cup of coffee"—a short stretch, kid, pretty decent, not bad at all, but back to the minors you go. But no matter, Uncle Rico and I would sit in the right field bleachers, enjoying the sun, eating peanuts, and watching Bobby play.

Those baseball years were so innocent and such very happy ones, among the happiest of my life. So, of course, it all had to end.

I was twelve when I met my first curve ball and fourteen when I hung up my cap, glove, and cleats. In those two years, playing for a variety of teams, I'd swing and miss, and miss, and miss almost every curve thrown my way.

I adjusted my grip, moving my hands an inch from the knob for better bat control. I tried to be more patient, delaying my swing until I knew where the ball was going. I tinkered with my stance—lead foot closer to the plate, lead foot away. I held my bat high. I held my bat low. But when it came to actually hitting the curve, nothing worked.

Fastballs were no problem. High speed, inside corner, low and outside, no problem. As long as the ball moved in a straight line, I was good: coiled and focused and ready to power the ball to deep center field or to left.

George, a catcher on all of those teams, watched my struggle with this devil pitch and said I should try something different.

"Like what?" I asked.

"Like move up in the batter's box and nail that mutha' just as it breaks."

I'd seen George do it with great success. I nodded. "I'll give it a try."

Sure enough, in the next game after moving up in the box, I blooped a slow curve at the start of its downward break to right field.

"Way to go, man!" George screamed. "You bad. You got it down, brother."

Maybe I had, I thought, as I raced to first.

My happy evaluation was premature. We played more games that season with more at bats, more curves, more swings and misses. Near the end, I wondered what had gone wrong, and I thought about that first curve, the only one I had ever managed to hit.

In my mind, I replayed the video, frame by frame. There was the ball leaving the pitcher's hand and me watching it move forward with its telltale spin, then beginning its slow-motion parachute-like descent, as if to say, "Hit me, pal, I'm your perfect pitch. Sure, I may be a curve, but I'm the friendliest, slowest curve you'll ever meet. And this afternoon, I'm served to you on a platter. Even you, puny batsman, even you can hit me."

The other curves were not as accommodating.

The best ones danced the mambo, zigged and zagged, and broke sharply. Against these curves, I was out of my league. I understood that this pitch would forever be my nemesis, my lurking vengeful antagonist, my existential threat.

I knew that as I got older and the pitchers got better, it would only get worse. By midseason I'd made my decision: I would quit playing baseball. It wasn't easy, and I dithered, changing my mind several times. Maybe offseason batting practice facing a steady diet of curves. Or how about a new pair of glasses. Maybe that would work.

Or maybe not.

In the last game of the season in my final at bat, I thought of Ted Williams, the Red Sox legend who'd homered in 1960 in the last at bat of his career. I wanted to go out the same way.

In the bottom of the last inning, I got my chance. My team was behind 1-0, but we had runners on second and third, two outs. A hit to the outfield would bring them home and give us the win.

The first pitch was a fastball inside corner. I swung and smashed a line drive over the third baseman's head, but the ball skipped just outside the line.

Strike one.

The second pitch, another fastball, was a little low but on the outside corner. A blooper to the right? I swung and missed.

I called time and stepped out of the box and took a deep breath. *Relax*, I told myself. *You got this. Relax.* I took a few swings and signaled to the ump I was ready to go.

I saw the pitch early, a curve, but it was moving inside, rib cage high. I leaned back as it suddenly broke down and over the inside corner of the plate.

"Stee-rike three," I heard the ump bellow. "You're outta here."

I turned and stared at the umpire, then muttered a curse, tossed my bat, gathered my jacket, and walked slowly off the field.

In retrospect, the end of the game foreshadowed several chapters of my life yet to unfold. Like so much of what I'd be part of over the years, even those very important moments—the end of my first marriage, my loss of faith, the end of a romance, the death of parents and close friends, my own first death—my baseball career ended, just like that.

Without a bang, not even a whimper.

UNCLE RICO'S ENCORE

saw my Uncle Rico on Friday, the day that he died.

My wife saw him on Saturday.

Wynona and I had just come in from San Francisco, taking shifts, gulping coffee, and driving all night to get to Seattle on time. We would have come earlier, but I was broke.

"Your uncle, this time it's serious," Mom had told me on the phone. "He wants to see you."

"Tell him to wait a few days," I said. "Until payday."

"But—"

"He's my uncle, he'll understand," I said. "He'll wait."

Rico waited.

We arrived on Friday afternoon, the VA hospital. Rico was shriveled and pale and not the stocky, muscular man who had helped raise me.

I kissed him on his forehead. "I love you, Uncle Rico," I said. "Thank you for being so good to me."

He blinked and smiled but couldn't respond. He was struggling to breathe.

Wynona took a towel and softly dabbed the corner of his mouth, where drool had formed. "I love you, Uncle," she said.

"And he loves you, too," I said softly.

Rico was fond of Wynona. "She's pretty," he once told me. "Nice."

Left unsaid was that she may have reminded him of his Chinatown female companions over the years, one in particular, a young dark-haired biracial woman who resembled my wife. Of her, he was especially fond, especially doting, until her pimp took her to Portland to dance on tables.

Uncle Rico had fallen asleep, his life down to hours, maybe less. We turned to look, then turned to leave. He was now beyond prayers, comforting wishes, healing words.

At that moment I was flooded by vivid memories—of Uncle Rico visiting our house when I was five, of us sitting outside on the concrete steps in the late afternoon sun, of him petting Joe, our dog, then rolling up his sleeve to show me a scar on his bicep.

"What's that?" I asked.

"Japanese bullet," he said.

"Were you scared?"

"No."

Then there was Rico and I in Chinatown, with me in tow. As always, he was impeccably dressed when we left his room on the second floor to wander up and down Jackson and King.

Years later, I'd return the favor and take him to lunch or dinner at the best Chinese or Filipino restaurants. Over dumplings or a plate of roast pork and garlic wings, we'd kill time, just giggling and talking—him in his broken English, me in my bad Bisayan. I don't remember what we said, or if we said anything at all, but none of that mattered.

For me, it was time well spent with someone I loved— good times, the best.

And finally, much earlier images, faded photo album black-and-whites when Rico and my dad first came to this land in the 1920s. They were so young, barely out of their teens. But even then, Dad and Rico were handsome and stylish, favoring shirts with flared collars and high-waisted, pleated slacks.

"Like a movie star," Rico said.

I nodded.

When I first met my uncle he was balding. Forty years later he was bald. But in one photo, he was sporting a pencil-thin mustache and a full thick head of black wavy hair, his sturdy arms folded across his chest, staring intently at the camera. Handsome. Dangerous. Seductive. No wonder that over the years, a steady stream of women—professional and willing volunteers—walked up the stairs, opened the door, and entered his room.

Yeah, I thought, *like a movie star.*

✦

After we left the VA, Wynona and I got in the car for the long ride back. I took a deep breath and gripped the steering wheel. The pressure was finally off. We could now take our time. No work until Monday. No drinking coffee black, no night racing through the Siskiyous, no stopping just to pee.

That evening, we pulled into a rundown motel near Medford. "I-5's Best Rates," the sign bragged. And no wonder. I got what I paid for—a cigarette-smelling room with flickering lights, scurrying roaches, lumpy mattress, thread-bare towels. But on my budget, I couldn't complain.

Once inside I called Mom. "How's Uncle . . ."

I could hear her crying. "He's gone," she whispered.

"When?"

"The nurse said maybe ten minutes after you left."

I closed my eyes. "He waited," I said.

"He waited."

On Saturday evening we were back in Frisco, in our apartment. The entire day had been untypically hot, and the heat still lingered. Wynona, who managed the units, was sitting at a desk next to the kitchen, writing receipts. I was in the living room, reclining on a couch next to a fan whirring fast and bringing relief.

Because of the heat, the door to the hallway was open. The apartment was finally getting cooler and I was exhausted, about to doze off, when Wynona approached me.

"In the hallway," she began. "I saw this man."

"Probably a tenant," I said sleepily, bringing up my legs and stretching out. I took a deep breath and smiled. *Nap time*, I thought. It's cooler now. Perfect.

"No, no, no," she said firmly. "I've never seen him before. Ever." Her sharp, urgent tone said listen close. I sat up and rubbed my eyes.

"Well, okay, okay, so what?"

"He was a young Filipino."

"So what? This town's full of 'em. You can't walk a block without bumping into one."

Wynona sighed. "You don't understand. I'm serious. He was just standing there and smiling, just like he knew me. Then I blinked, and he was gone." She looked away, as if to gather her thoughts. "I rushed to the doorway and looked up and down the hall. Empty. No sign. No sound of footsteps. Gone."

I yawned and stretched. "Maybe it's the heat, the long drive, you being tired, maybe all three, and sometimes the imagination can . . ."

She ignored me. "He was stocky, not too tall but handsome with thick black hair, very well dressed but in an old-fashioned way, like a gangster from one of those 1930s movies."

Very well dressed but old-fashioned, I thought. *Maybe* . . .

"Tell me about the hair," I said.

"Thick and—"

"Wavy?"

She nodded. I shuddered.

"And one other thing," she said. "He had this—"

"Mustache," I said.

"Yes."

"Uncle Rico," I said. "He liked you, and he didn't want you to remember him in his last minutes, shrunken, helpless, and drooling."

My heart raced. Breathe in, hold, push out. Repeat.

"My uncle," I finally said. "He was a proud man. He wanted you to see him as handsome and well dressed, what he used to be." I smiled as those old photo album black-and-whites flashed in my mind. "He wanted you to know he looked like Cagney."

"Who?"

"Jimmy Cagney, an old-time actor," I said. I paused. "A movie star."

THE DEBT

"The O'Dea Irish scoring record," Brother J. B. Jones said calmly. "Hey, Bacho, you're gonna own it when you're done."

I stared at Brother Jones. This was a message I never expected to hear. He was serious, not a hint of a smile, like this was a truth he had to tell me.

I liked Brother Jones, trusted him and his basketball instincts. He knew the game, honed by years of high school and street ball in New York City, the home of the legendary Lou Alcindor and the center of the basketball world. Our months together as coach and player had made us close. I didn't know then that he was planning to leave O'Dea and the Irish Christian Brothers in just a few months.

"You mean it?" I asked.

He nodded. "Yes, I do."

"Dang."

Every fifteen-year-old has acne and self-doubt, and I had my share of both. At that age we're fragile but curious. I was an especially fragile one—an introvert, just average in the classroom, mute and awkward around girls. Sports, by default, became my outlet, my one area of confident expression and success, basketball in particular.

At some point the luckier ones will have a trusted adult say, "Kid, you can make it. You've got talent." At a key juncture the trajectory of young lives can be made by the right words, or broken by the wrong ones.

I was at that juncture. And thanks to Brother Jones, I was lucky. Our conversation took place in March 1965, after our freshman basketball season. With a win over hated rival Seattle Prep, we were Seattle's Catholic school champions. I was a starting forward on that team, skin and bones skinny, but with a nice jump shot, an array of deft head feints, and a quick first step to the hole.

J. B. Jones was our coach. When I returned to school in September, he was gone. Just like that. I asked one of the brothers what happened to him.

He shrugged. "He left the order," he said and sighed. "This kind of life, it can be hard, laddie, and it's not for everyone."

"Do you know where he is?"

"Last I heard, he's back in New York. I think."

"Brother, do you have an address?"

"No."

I was stunned. Like my parents and uncles, Brother Jones had helped to shape me. And I didn't have a chance to thank him or to even say goodbye. It's a regret I carry with me to this day.

Over the next two years I toiled away in obscurity, playing on the junior varsity through my sophomore and junior years in meaningless games. As a player, I was just going through the motions.

But the varsity coach, an unimaginative sort, didn't believe in playing undergraduates. I chafed and for a moment thought about packing it in and transferring to another high school. I was daydreaming about the chance to play in varsity games in packed gyms, get write-ups in the local papers, maybe meet a girl, and maybe, just maybe, catch the eye of a curious college scout.

As a JV baller, I knew none of that was going to happen.

I stayed at O'Dea partly because of Brother Jones, but there were other reasons as well. My teammates and I were friends, close friends, and many of us had played on that championship freshman team, an experience that bonded us. During this time I never hinted to any of them that I considered playing at another school. They would see it as a betrayal, and I would have agreed. It was a guilt I didn't want to bear.

"We'll get our chance," I told Stan one day after JV practice. He was a skilled, long-limbed, athletic guard on our freshman team.

Stan sighed. "This waitin' stuff, man, I hope so," he said.

Then there was a final reason as well: my intense dislike of rich guys. And in the 1960s, Seattle Prep was full of them, the privileged and smug sons of doctors, lawyers, business leaders, and the like. For them, the teenage years were easy. And life beyond high school? No sweat. Decades of success? It's in their DNA.

In those days Seattle Prep drew most of its students from the tony white enclaves of Capitol Hill and Madison

Park and the wealthier parishes north of the Montlake Bridge. O'Dea, with its much lower tuition, attracted boys from working-class and poorer neighborhoods—the Central Area, the South End, West Seattle, and White Center. A few came from the projects.

Prep's student body was almost all white; O'Dea's wasn't.

But far worse was Prep's athletic success in the 1960s. The school fielded strong, competitive basketball squads and unbeaten state champion football teams with full rosters and major college recruits. Year in and year out, in the great Seattle Catholic school rivalry, it was the same old story.

But as rivalries go, it wasn't much of one. In those two sports, Prep teams would take the field or basketball court and squash O'Dea. The outcomes were routine, expected. Seattle Prep versus O'Dea? No stop-the-press news stories there. All that money plus athletic success, it just didn't seem fair.

At sixteen, I kept hearing Billie Holiday's voice: "Them that's got shall get, them that's not shall lose, so the Bible says and it still is news." It kept playing in my mind, haunting me. I couldn't shake it. A lyrical metaphor for life? For my life?

Damn, I hoped not.

I resolved to do my best to hone my skills and change the script. During my senior year, we'd beat Seattle Prep in a game that mattered. It became my singular focus, my unhealthy obsession, thought about during the day, dreamed about at night.

For me, it became the only thing in my life that mattered. Never mind finding a girlfriend. Never mind the young Pinoys I knew who were getting drafted and sent to Vietnam, some not to return. Never mind that I could be next.

The summer before my senior year, 1967, I played ball almost every day at Madrona Elementary School, not too far from my home. There were two hoops on the asphalt playground, and that's where the best players in the city gathered. All were Black, except for me. Most were recent graduates of Garfield High, Seattle's basketball power-house. Some were already playing for junior college and college teams.

All could play. All took the games seriously.

At Madrona, basketball was a blood sport. Physical con-tact on each play was a given. No harm—at least not bone-jutting-through-the-skin harm—no foul. The reticent and well-mannered need not apply.

Three-man teams would play a half-court game. One point a basket. The scoring team kept possession. The first to fifteen won—and kept playing.

At the start, I'd be the last one chosen, a foreigner, an unknown, un-Black commodity. But as the weeks passed, my game improved. I was driving quicker to the hole, bodying up—belly and chest on back—and defending tenaciously, jumping quicker and higher when I hit the boards, and nailing hooks and midrange and pull-up jumpers.

I was playing like a brother. After a few weeks, I stopped being the last one chosen. In their arrogance, soccer fans stand up and proclaim that their sport is the beautiful game. They're wrong. Basketball at Madrona was better.

One day in late August, I bumped into Cookie in down-town Seattle. He was leaning casually against a building being Cookie cool, toothpick in the side of his mouth, enjoy-ing the late afternoon sun and eyeing the women walking by in their shorts and thin summer dresses. He was maybe twenty-five, 6'3", 245 pounds of Black muscle and pure athletic ability. At Madrona no one messed with Cookie.

He saw me first. "Hey, man," he said. "I thought we beat you off the court."

"Nah, Cookie, you didn't."

He smiled. "Maybe we didn't."

✦

Two more weeks of summer. I had a tough time sleeping, so eager was I for the school year to start. I looked forward to spending every day after class in the gym, shooting jumper after jumper, running sprints and stairs until my legs burned and my eyes bugged out, scrimmaging hard and getting ready for the season and the full-court game. The months at Madrona made me quicker, more aggressive, far more confident.

This would be the year, I told myself, *we'd finally beat Seattle Prep.*

After a scrimmage, my friend Stan walked up to me. "Your game," he said. "It got better."

"Thanks," I said. "I worked real hard." I paused. "We're gonna get 'em this year," I said.

"Who?"

"Who else."

"Prep?"

"Who else."

✦

The season finally started in early December. We started well, winning two out of our first three games, then went into a monthlong tailspin. And no wonder. The schedule was brutal. We played three games a week—Tuesday, Friday, and Saturday. I remember one week in particular, when we went on the road to play an excellent Aberdeen High School team on Friday, then drove back the entire 109 miles to Seattle to face dangerous and very physical Central Kitsap at home Saturday.

We were trounced both times.

Looking back more than fifty years later, our December performance still rankles me. It didn't have to be that way. But it's small wonder we were so bad. Only two players had any minutes of varsity experience, mostly bench time and sometimes a handful of mop-up minutes. We had talent, sure, but we had to learn how to play as a varsity team against much tougher competition. We spent December doing that, incurring more losses and our coach's wrath.

During halftime of one sorry game, the coach was drawing Xs and Os on the blackboard. He suddenly turned, red faced and beady eyed, to look at me. He exploded.

"Damn it, Bacho, you don't listen!" Coach screamed, and threw a piece of chalk at me.

I ducked, and the chalk sailed past my ear. It was a Bobby Knight moment; at least he didn't throw a chair. I kept calm and thought, *You're right, asshole, I've stopped listening.*

And I think we all did.

We played the remaining games for each other and began to play more smoothly; hard-learned experience was starting to kick in. I went back to how I played at Madrona— aggressive, willing to take chances, unafraid of making mistakes, getting yelled at, and getting benched.

And in January the team began to turn around. We started with a road win at Central Kitsap, the team that had beaten us so handily just weeks before. In those days the best of the

Catholic schools would play against the third-place Seattle public school team, with the winner advancing to the state tournament. And although Prep squeaked by us in the first game, we weren't discouraged. We ran off two straight wins against Blanchet, a recent state champion and our other Catholic rival, which did us a favor by beating Prep.

This set the stage for the last game, a February 23, winner-take-all showdown between O'Dea and Prep. In the first quarter we jumped out early to a big lead and never let up. By the end of the first half, the outcome was no longer in doubt. When the game ended, our fans stormed the court and carried us off.

"Irish End Frustration," the *Seattle Times* headline read the following day. Above the story was a photo of our center, Mike Walls, grabbing a rebound. The ball is pressed against his chest, his expression fierce, his elbows angled out and sharp, weaponized. He looked like the great Bill Russell, Mike's idol.

Russell could not have done it better. "Take it from me if you can!" the photo screamed.

After the game Mike and I and a couple of our class-mates got in a car and drove around the city, savoring the win and feeling that for this one special night the city belonged to us. We stopped in an empty lot in Ballard. I got out, stretched my back, took a deep breath and screamed.

I returned to the car and looked at Mike. "We did it," I said.

He nodded and smiled. "What's next?"

I shook my head, thinking, *After this game? After this season? After this year? After college? After the draft, the army, and Vietnam?*

"I'll think about it tomorrow," I said.

◆

The older I get, the more precious, the more pristine some memories become. As I've aged, I've forgotten entire chapters and significant chunks of time: almost all of grade school, earlier marriages, most affairs, my first two years of college. I am sure there are others. But I've chosen to retain moments that have meant the most.

Beating Seattle Prep was one of those.

◆

It is the first of the month, and I am sitting in the kitchen in my most comfortable chair writing checks. I make one out to O'Dea High School. In the lower left-hand corner is a "For" and a line.

"Brother Jones," I write on the line. "1965."

SEPTEMBER 20, 1968

C ould it really have been that long ago?

The first day of my eighteenth year and I am spending it at the military induction center in Seattle. Me and other accidental boy soldiers, filling out forms, taking tests, bending over, just bobbing along in a white Fruit of the Loom sea. I glanced around the room. Not many razors needed.

I was a product of Catholic schools, deferred sexuality, and stations-of-the-cross sublimation—a virgin. But I knew I wasn't the only one. I also knew that some of them weren't coming back. And on their tombstones it should read "Poor, poor [fill in the name]. The only tit he ever sucked was his mom's."

Was I scared? Too strong. Apprehensive? That fits.

My road to the induction center started the year before in the spring of 1967, when I got a phone call from a high school pal, Steve Aspiras. We were juniors at the time, and the Vietnam War was too far down the road to worry about. Besides, as a soon-to-be senior at O'Dea High, I had more important things to worry about, like a high hopes basketball season. Steve said he'd drive, and we'd be joined by Ted Divina, Vince Visaya, and Gene Navarro, the other three slightly older than Steve and me, their high school years a chapter in their past.

As we cruised the city's neighborhoods and headed downtown, we listened to R & B, just hanging out—an activity at which Filipino Americans of my day excelled. Among the jokes and banter, the camaraderie, the comfort that comes with a common ethnic identity and a shared history, Gene suddenly dropped a bomb.

He'd signed with the Marines, he said, his tone matter-of-fact. He'd be reporting to boot camp in a few days. Ted and Vince would be next, snatched up by the military. For all three, there was only one destination: Vietnam.

That's when the war hit home. My time was coming.

Gene, Vince, and Ted could have postponed military service by going to college, with its life-saving four-year draft deferment. I was hoping to do that. But among too many of my Filipino peers, it wasn't an option. Our immigrant parents came from poverty; in America they worked in the nation's underbelly, migrating to seasonal backbreaking jobs on farms and in salmon canneries. The luckier ones worked as busboys and dishwashers. By the 1960s their economic situation had improved, but not enough to send their sons to college.

My friends also had unconsidered options, like Canada. But I know what they would have said. *Nope, that's what white guys did.* Or how about growing their hair, burning their draft cards, and protesting the war. Same thing.

Then there was the stereotype, prevalent among Seattle's white public high school teachers and counselors, that unlike studious and well-behaved Japanese and Chinese boys—*yes sir, no sir, three bags full sir*—young Filipino males were just not college material. Try the post office, they were told, or learn a trade. Oh, and cut your hair, stop jaywalking, and pay taxes.

They smoked, they drank, they talked smack to the ladies and slicked their hair, Pomade, of course, just like their dads. They brawled in the streets. They danced too Black. College? In 1967? Gimme a break, brotha' man. That's what white guys did.

It's not like Vietnam was the only thing I thought about. But when I did I had a hard time seeing myself in army green. For starters, I hated the woods, never mind swamps, steamy jungles, rice paddies, killer snakes, and pooping outside. Ditto for hiking and sleeping outdoors. Guns and loud noises scared me. Getting shot scared me more. Campfires without s'mores? Forget it.

I felt lucky being not yet seventeen, which gave me more than a year of ongoing adolescence and perhaps enough time to figure things out. Besides, maybe the war would be over by then. Plus there were the distractions of senior year: the upcoming basketball season, college applications, and with a little luck, maybe even a girlfriend.

Everything but the girlfriend went okay. We beat Seattle Prep, our bitter crosstown rival, and qualified for the playoffs, where we got bounced in the first game. I even got accepted, despite an exceedingly modest academic record, to the University of Washington. But a girlfriend? I fell one win short of the triple crown.

Graduation came and went, and I was three months away from turning eighteen. It was time to get serious about this Vietnam thing, a point driven home by our Filipino summer league basketball team. As the season wore on, our guys kept disappearing, leaving for basic. Leaving for war.

Then one day in August, I decided to launch a preemptive strike. I would join the army, but only under my terms. Sure, I had been accepted by the UW. My acceptance gave me the precious deferment. But how long I could hold onto it was another matter. The truth was that going to the university intimidated me. It was so impersonal, bloodless, soulless and huge, a city within a city, and I was convinced I would flunk out and become meat for the body-hungry draft and, like so many draftees, be sent to the bush to hike and shoot and poop outdoors.

I told the recruiter I wanted to be in military intelligence, where my ability to type and answer telephones, follow office etiquette, and politely brownnose superiors would be highly valued. I also wanted the six-month delayed entry program, my Plan B after flunking out of the UW.

He tried to talk me into the airborne. No thanks, I replied. I signed the paperwork, and on my birthday I reported to the induction center.

At the end of what was becoming a tedious day, I had one more step in the process: a meeting with the medical officer. In a sense I was relieved. This day would finally end, Plan B would be under way, and it would have been too, but earlier I had filled out a form asking if I had a history of the listed maladies or diseases.

"Asthma," I wrote, which was true. As a child, I'd even been hospitalized after a nasty attack. But I outgrew it and became the picture of teenage health, playing football in the fall, basketball in the winter, and baseball in the spring.

I entered the doc's office. He was seated behind his desk, and he motioned for me to sit down. As he scanned my medical history, I glanced at his features: blond hair with blue eyes, a handsome man who looked younger than his calendar years. He also looked kind, serene, like a priest who'd just been sitting at the right hand of God.

He looked up and stared at me. "I see you've had asthma," he said solemnly.

"Yes, I had it as a child—"

"That means if you go to a hot dusty place there's a chance your asthma could act up."

Hmm, I hadn't thought of that. My asthma acting up in a hot, dusty, and violent environment was the least of my worries. I was puzzled, unsure what the doc was getting at. Before I could reply, he repeated himself, slower and more firmly this time, like he was talking to an idiot: "That . . . means . . . if . . . you . . . go . . . to . . . a . . . hot . . . dusty . . . place . . ."

Ding. I realized he was trying to flunk me out. He was doing his best to give me my life.

"Yeah," I mumbled. "Sure."

He sat back in his chair, the slightest of smiles forming at the corners of his mouth. "I'm afraid you can't join the army, son. Sorry. You'll get a 1-Y instead."

"A 1-Y?"

"It means you'll only serve if there's a national emergency."

I got up to leave. This was so unexpected, I didn't know what to feel.

Half a century later, I can't remember if I thanked him then, but I now know I should have. Because of that doc, I was able to continue in college, go to law school, and screw up a legal career and two out of three marriages.

But why the kindness? Maybe it was because he knew that the war couldn't be won, or maybe it was proof that God really does love fools, or perhaps it was because the great cosmic joker, Senor Lucky Dog, chose my birthday to drop me a bone. Or maybe it all went deeper—that he knew the war shouldn't have been fought in the first place. Whatever the reason, I know he concluded that I'd be one more teenage discardable in this most dubious of battles.

Ah, but the doc didn't know of Plan B—that I'd carefully planned to sit out my tour in an office with air conditioning, or at least fans. But being eighteen and very naïve, I didn't realize that my best laid plan could *gang aft agley*—easy enough in a war zone.

Every morning for the last several years, I've smudged with tobacco and sage, praying for the well-being of those who are close to me. When his turn comes up, I see his face.

This is my prayer: "Thank you, army doc who saved my life."

IRMA

—

After two boys, Mom desperately wanted a girl. And that's what she got when Irma was born.

My sister's birth mercifully put an end Mom's deep yearnings and at least one cockamamie scheme involving a 1957 road trip to Frisco. The objective: to ask Lydia, her favorite niece, and Ben, her husband, to give her Dinah, the second daughter with the big brown eyes.

Recently, Dinah told me the story freshly pulled from our family's vault. I remembered, then nodded and laughed.

"Yeah, that's Mom," I said. "True enough." In my mind, I can see Mom and Lydia sitting at the kitchen table. I can hear their voices. I can hear the conversation.

"Hoy, Lydia," Mom said soothingly. "You still got Mildred. Oh, and don't forget, there's Bobby. You got him, too. But this second one, ah, too many, don't you think? And besides, you're young, so there's more on the way. No doubt about that." Mom paused. "After a while, you won't even know she's gone."

I can see Lydia, hands folded, head nodding, her eyes bouncing wildly in her skull. What to say?

What to say? And of course, Lydia punted. "I'll have to ask Ben," she said.

And, of course, Ben said no, this is crazy.

So Operation Extract Dinah failed, but that's not the point. My mother, so kind and polite, had a way of making the absurd seem reasonable. Hers was a pre-Marvel superpower.

Like a few summers later, we were again visiting Lydia. This time the house was packed with our small family (five, including Irma) and her growing brood (three new kids, plus parents, eight in all). We were all asleep when suddenly Mom woke us up and assembled us in the living room.

"Hoy," I remember her solemnly saying. "Tonight, there are thirteen people asleep in this house. And you know what that means." She paused and looked at me. "Peter, grab your blanket. Go sleep in the car."

"But Auntie," Dinah said, as she stretched and yawned. "Millie's not here. She went clubbin' and won't be back . . ."

Bobby, increasingly the target of Millie's wall-piercing caterwauls, smirked. "Till she gets some—"

Dinah turned toward her brother, her eyes throwing darts stopping his sentence. "She won't be back until noon," Dinah said blandly. "So now we've got twelve, right?" She paused, yawning. "So, Auntie, I think that means we're okay."

Mom, brow furrowed, scanned the room counting noses. She smiled and nodded. No Millie, sure enough. "Go back to bed," Mom said.

For my mother, San Francisco was a beautiful city, a magical place, made doubly so by the presence of Lydia and her family. I thought at the time that maybe this happy convergence—this perfect storm of metaphysical forces—drove Mom to say really nutty things.

Then maybe not, because back home in Seattle, she was more than able to riff on her own. Like the time she told me she planned to get her hands on Ferdinand Marcos's hidden gold stash, which once belonged to General MacArthur, who had taken it from the Japanese, who, of course, had taken it from Filipinos during the occupation.

Never mind that she was living in Seattle and that she hadn't been back to the Philippines in decades and detested Marcos but not his ill-gotten loot.

She told me her plan on a late Saturday afternoon. We were sitting across from each other—a corner booth, a smoky Chinatown dive—picking at the surviving noodles of a tasty chow mein. She tilted her head back and blinked, Mom's sign to please move closer, she had something to say.

I leaned forward, inching within whispering range. "My second cousin has a friend named Inday. I met her the other day."

"And?"

"I trust her," Mom continued. "She has kind eyes, even teeth. You know what that means? She can pay the dentist, a good sign. So, no doubt in my mind, Inday comes from money. A famous street in Cebu, why, it's named after her grandfather." Mom paused. "She's got no reason to steal."

Another pause. Mom looked at me, waiting for her persuasion to sink in. "Her brother is a major and he knows where McCoy's—"

"McCoy?"

From my mother, furrowed eyes, a stern look. "We're in public," she whispered. "You don't know who's listening."

From me, a sigh of resignation. "They're new immigrants, Mom, FOBs from Hong Kong. They speak Cantonese, not English."

She looked around. "Shh. McCoy. Remember, McCoy," she whispered. "We'll just call him that."

I shrugged. "Okay, okay, McCoy then," I said.

Mom smiled. "Like I said, her brother knows—"

"And so, let me guess, Mom. For a small fee—"

"Five thousand," she said calmly. "Equipment, crew, bribes, security, that sort of thing. When she gets the gold, we'll split it fifty-fifty."

Grifter alert. My eyes narrowed. "Five thousand," I tried to say calmly. "And you gave her the money?"

"Sure. It was part of the deal."

"But Mom, you're about to retire, and how could you—"

"Shh."

I started to cough, too much smoke, too much aggravation. It was time to leave. I signaled the waiter and paid the tab. Mom and I walked outside as a jetliner flew overhead in the blue, cloudless late afternoon sky.

"Mom, this McCoy stuff, it's just crazy."

Mom shrugged. "You'll see," she said.

"And besides, how can you afford . . ."

Mom gazed skyward tracking the plane—her face pious, peaceful, and content—a Michelangelo cherub. In Bisayan her whispered prayer, the sign of the cross.

"Boeing stock," she said softly. "I sold some."

GUILT

———

As a child, guilt was the jet-powered fuel that drove me.

I couldn't escape it, especially when I was kneeling during mass, gazing at the crucifix, listening to the sermon, and, especially during Holy Week, pondering Christ's suffering and the role my sins and numerous imperfections played in His death.

In 1958, Pope Pius XII died, and over the next several weeks I couldn't escape the feeling that I, at eight years old, somehow must have been responsible for his demise. Sixty years later, I'm still befuddled at how I reached that conclusion.

Despite the Pope's death, life went on. No one I knew fainted or cried inconsolably. Dad went to work, Mom went to beauty school, and I went to Saint Teresa's. I have no doubt that the nuns and my classmates didn't bear my burden.

Looking back, I'm not sure what misfiring synapse in my undeveloped brain, what rogue DNA led me to believe what I believed, but it did. Maybe, and unbeknown to the younger me, I had powerful telekinetic powers, allowing me to send death rays to kill a doddering old man thousands of miles away.

Or perhaps Pope Pius had a vision that years from now I would abruptly leave the church and become a libertine, a mass-avoiding, free-thinking, first-ballot-unanimous vote hall-of-fame sinner, and the knowing just killed him.

My growing suspicion that I'd caused the Holy Father's death led to a string of sleepless nights, uneaten meals, and distracted days. It led to hours of prayer, in church and on my knees at the foot of my bed, begging for forgiveness.

"Forgive me, God," I'd pray. "I'm so sorry. I didn't mean to do it."

Over the next several days, my suspicion hardened into a conviction that I, indeed, was the culprit. My crime led me to the confessional.

"Bless me Father," I began.

"Yes, my son."

"I think I killed Pope Pius."

"You what?"

"I said, Father, I'm the one. I'm the murderer. I killed Pope Pius."

Through the black screen separating penitent from priest, I could hear him sigh. I could also see him slowly shake his head and raise his hand, massaging his temple with his fingers. "Jesus Christ," I heard him whisper. "I need a drink. What the hell . . ."

Hmm, I thought, *that didn't sound like a prayer*. "Father?"

He cleared his throat and sighed again.

"Father?"

"Yes, my son," he said softly.

"Father . . ."

"The Holy Father was quite old," he began. "It was his time, that's all, and our Lord called him to be with Him." The priest paused. "You're innocent. You had nothing to do with his death. You've committed no sin."

"I didn't commit a sin?"

"No, my son."

I blinked, for a moment disbelieving the good news. "Father, are you sure?"

"Yes."

"Yay."

✦

During my eight years at Saint Teresa and my four years at O'Dea, I continued to go to mass and to confess my sins. It was a weekly routine—confession on Saturday, mass on Sunday. And I loved it so much I served as an altar boy. The rituals and beliefs of Catholicism gave me a structure, solid enough for me to believe that God and I were always on the same page.

But then trouble arose.

When I reached the eighth grade, I had a new sin to confess: impure thoughts inspired by women and girls modeling modest one-piece swimwear in the Sears catalog—their legs, calves, and ankles were of particular adolescent fascination. With great vigor, I would shake my head, hoping that the motion would dislodge the thoughts from my brain, where they'd seep through my skull, float silently through the air, and find a new home in the mind of another unsuspecting boy.

I heard one priest say that lustful thoughts were mortal sins. They were surefire tickets to the eternal fires of hell, he declared, as heinous as divorce, murder, fornication, masturbation, infidelity, and eating pork chops on Friday.

I did not want to go to hell.

My physical response to these thoughts would sometimes embarrass me, like the afternoon my friend George and I were walking home from baseball practice. As usual, we were taking our time and talking about baseball.

"You'll hit the curve, my man, don't worry," he said. "I watched you swing the bat. Smooth, brother, more confident. Now you're timing the break and making contact, you're closer." He paused and looked at me, making sure, like the good friend he was, that I got his message. "I can tell. You're closer."

"Thanks, George." I started to shake my head at the sudden, uninvited image of a smiling young blonde's ankle, calf, and thigh.

"Man, you okay?"

"Yeah," I said. "I got this condition, asthma, and my mom gave me these pills, and sometimes the pills cause . . ."

George nodded. His eyes narrowed in focus and commiseration. "Dang, I'm glad I don't have asthma."

"Yeah, you're lucky."

For a string of Saturday afternoons, I confessed to the presence of impure thoughts until Father Marsh, my weekly confessor, tired of my litany of sinful thoughts.

"You're innocent and pure," he said. "You just aren't capable of committing a mortal sin. My son, it's just not who you are."

Damn, was he wrong.

When I finally did leave the safe bosom of the church, I was in my early twenties and, ironically, I had even earned an undergraduate degree in theology from a Catholic university. The decision wasn't easy. I'd been the perfect Catholic baby, born to a deeply religious mother and an irreligious but go-along-to-get-along father.

On matters of religion, Dad just nodded. "It's up to your mom," he'd say.

My entire life had been wrapped around a self-contained system of thinking, acting, and believing—a complete, self-sustaining ecosystem. For believers, any question raised would always have an infallible answer.

I told myself then that I left because of a crisis of faith, my discovery of Pius XII's criminal passivity in the slaughter of Jews during World War II, not to mention the earlier wars, pogroms, crusades, and persecutions launched or inspired by the Vatican.

Wow, that sounded good—a profound, historically based, deeply principled reason my still-practicing friends could disagree with but accept.

But here's the truth: Mostly I left for other less safe bosoms.

Whatever the reason, I have no regrets about leaving the church.

I don't miss attending mass, confessing my sins, or praying the rosary and novenas. I don't miss the stations of the cross, ushers collecting tithes, holy water signs of the cross, standing, sitting, kneeling in my pew, and inhaling incense.

I don't miss hearing Latin and later the sounds of strumming guitars and earnest but off-key singing.

I don't miss the church.

The last fifty years have been mostly guilt free.

Sure, there were moments of guilt, just not of the Catholic kind.

✦

I loved my late mother, Remedios, and she loved me. Ours was a special, sacred bond. But that didn't stop her from yanking my invisible umbilical chain when she saw the need arise.

"Don't forget, you're the oldest," Mom told me after one of my many lapses. "You will always have an obligation."

"For what, Mom."

"To do right. To make it work. To set an example."

I remember one day in particular, a Thursday night near the end of the quarter. I was living in Tacoma then and teaching at the University of Washington branch campus.

I was relaxed, ready to go to bed, but then the telephone rang. I picked up the receiver. I should not have answered.

"Manong Peter," my sister Irma said. "I bought you a ticket for Reno. A morning flight. Seven, okay?"

"Huh?"

Irma explained that Norris, the middle sibling, was in trouble again. He'd been a high-ranking city official but had had a very public fallout with his bosses. Now he was in jail, busted for forging drug prescriptions. Irma had tried to find him a lawyer, but no one wanted the job.

Irma's husband Lio, she said, would meet me in the terminal with the ticket and enough money to bail Norris out and to find an attorney.

I took a depth breath. I've always had a hard time saying no to my sister.

"I can't, Irma," I finally said. "I've still got all these papers to read. Then there's finals coming up next week. And besides that, for most of his life he was always screwin' up, and the family's always bailed him out." I paused. "Always," I said, my voice starting to rise. "But not this time, baby. No way. This mess ain't on me. It ain't on us."

"Manong Peter," Irma whined.

"No."

Then my mother got on the line. She was crying.

"Mom."

"Pee-tair," she said between sobs. "He's your only brah-dair."

Damn, I thought. A mother-sister double team. This ain't even fair.

✦

It's 7:30 the next day. I'm doing what I usually do, sipping coffee and reading the *New York Times*. The flight is on schedule. I'm Reno bound.

ON BOXING, MOTHER, VIOLENCE, AND WRITING

VAN THE MAN

F rom 1979 to 1980, I finally learned how to fight.

A bunch of us trained in a tiny gym on the second floor of the Wallingford Boys Club in Seattle. It was little more than a small room, but it had a raised ring and several heavy bags. It was enough. We weren't by any measure elite boxers. No one would be competing to qualify for the Olympic team.

As a group, we were too old. We had jobs, marriages, careers. But no matter. Despite our age and even with headgear and large sparring gloves, and even at our low-rung level, the pain was real. The competition was real, especially when boxers from other clubs came to spar.

Those spars turned into wars.

The black eyes were real: ditto the cut lips, a broken nose, the stinging head shots, the crippling hooks to the solar plexus, the knockdowns and knockouts, and for one of us, years down the road, the onset of Parkinson's Disease.

The overall experience was both a blessing and a wonder no one got sued. To paraphrase the great Ray Robinson, boxing is a "hurting" sport. And our ringleader was a journeyman ex-pro and boxing coach extraordinaire, Van Taylor.

Years later, after we'd hung up our gloves, Van said, "Petah, Petah, Petah, you shoulda turned pro. We'da made some money."

In a life now spanning seventy years, it was the best compliment I've ever received.

✦

Right jab to the head, hard left counter to the body, right hook to the head, right foot outside his left, pivot to the right. Repeat.

This is what a southpaw does against a left-hand leading orthodox fighter, in this case a compact, muscular middleweight who was boring straight in. He was hoping to close the gap and take off my head with his power hand, his right.

But he was a plodder, strong but unimaginative, wholly predictable. By moving, pivoting, and maintaining distance, I never gave him the chance to land that punch or any other, for that matter.

That night, more than forty years ago, everything I threw landed. The first round ended, and I walked to my corner. I was pleased with myself, especially since my good friend Teddy and I had spent the afternoon drinking.

I glanced at Teddy, who was leaning against the wall. He smirked and turned away. Van was working my corner. As he toweled me down, his eyes narrowed.

"Homeboy, you been drinkin'," he said in a voice only I could hear.

I shrugged. "What should I do this round?"

Van just shook his head and grunted.

"Well?" The bell rang. I shrugged, then turned, raised my hands, and walked back to center ring.

"Do what you want," I heard him growl. "You don't listen no how."

Which was true.

It couldn't have been any other way. Van was an orthodox, left-lead fighter, a slugger with power in both hands. He was short and compact for a heavyweight, often fighting taller, longer, and heavier men. Success meant bobbing and weaving, slipping or blocking punches, and always shuffling forward just to get within range.

As a coach, I don't think Van knew what to do with evasive, skinny, long-necked southpaws like me. So when he gave me a tip, I'd nod politely and do something else.

But for me, our time together was valuable. The lessons I learned came from watching him work, how relentless he was, slipping and moving inside to punish his opponent with short, powerful punches. Up until then I'd been content to box, to stay back and rely on my long reach and quick hands and feet.

Safety first, I'd told myself. It's just a sport. A fight in a phone booth? No thank you, not for me. In those days, I was pain averse. Four decades later, I still am.

But my learning curve of fighting this way had its drawbacks, like me against shorter, thick-necked artless sluggers. They'd ignore my jabs and quick flurries and fancy footwork, cut off the ring, pin me against the ropes, and rip left hooks and straight rights to my kidneys, belly, and jaw.

I was determined to figure this out, to finally find an answer.

With Van, I worked on the unfamiliar skills of slipping and blocking and moving inside. I finally understood that dancing and being clever and using my array of long-range skills, pretty though they were, were often not enough against stronger, more determined, and aggressive fighters.

So I learned and adapted.

At some point early in a match, I would turn into Van. I would snort and disregard danger, walk in bobbing and weaving, and hit him hard enough to inflict pain, to rattle confidence and reduce aggression. Message delivered, I would then return to the style that I loved—moving quickly and gracefully, pivoting and setting traps to counterpunch, throwing quick pitty-pat punches, anticipating and slipping punches thrown in return.

In the hard sport of boxing, this is as close as I have come to creating art. But for me to do that, to box the way I wanted to, I had to become someone I wasn't to be someone I was.

This was a valuable lesson in and beyond the ring, and one I've kept with me to this day.

◆

I'd first met Van in 1979 at the University of Washington's Rec Center. In those days the center had a boxing ring, and Van was coaching the boxing club. I studied him closely and liked the way he treated his fighters, always stressing the basics of offense and defense and making sure each boxer wasn't overmatched when he faced an opponent.

Not being overmatched, that was a big thing for me, especially since I'd been in gyms where trainers tossed me and other beginners into the ring to spar three rounds against boxers with more skills and power.

We were fodder, little more than punching bags who had legs, moved, and felt and expressed pain. Some lasted the full three rounds; others didn't.

Next man up, a trainer would bark. Come on, come on. My guy, he's got a fight comin' up. Jesus Christ, people, he needs his rounds.

Van did none of that. I decided then that he would train me.

✦

Outside of the ring, Van and I became close friends, and over the months and years to follow, he told me his story. Aside from being a prizefighter, he'd also spent time robbing banks.

"Why?" I asked.

"My girlfriend's idea," he said. "Said I wasn't makin' enough as a fighter."

"And you went along?"

Van shrugged. "Until I got caught."

While he was in prison, he'd joined the Nation of Islam and had even changed his ring name from "Taylor" to "Sahib." But the spiritual significance of the name change lasted until his thirty-ninth birthday, when he and I sat down to breakfast at a downtown café to celebrate.

The waitress came over and looked at me.

"A cheese omelet," I said.

She turned to Van.

"Two eggs over easy and bacon, oh, and an extra side."

"Of bacon?"

"Yeah, baby, it's my birthday, and my friend here's payin'."

I looked at Van. "Hey, man, I thought you were Muslim."

He smiled. "Yeah, me, too."

But "Van Sahib" is how he's listed on the website Box-Rec: ten fights, four wins, six losses. Two of those losses were to highly skilled, dangerous fighters: Yaqui Lopez, a great light heavyweight and Hall of Fame inductee, and Ibar Arrington, a lanky, quick heavyweight with good movement and a punishing left jab. In the 1970s, Arrington fought the best heavyweights in boxing, including Larry Holmes, the reigning champ.

These were fights Van should never have taken. His record won't get him into the HOF, but it's one that needs correcting.

"I took a dive," he said casually, one lazy Saturday afternoon as we guzzled red wine. "But just one."

"Why?"

"I wouldn't be fightin' for big money. Sometimes me and my trainer, damn, we lucky to make expenses. Man, I knew that, and then some cat slips me some cash, so why not?" Van drank some more wine and shrugged.

I shrugged, too. "Yeah, why not," I said.

✦

I was at Van's last fight in 1979, in the high school gym in Sedro Wooley, a small Washington farming town close to the Canadian border. He was up against some guy I'd never heard of, just a body with a name, "Tim," penciled in to fill in the card.

For two months I'd been working with Van, trying to get him ready. We'd spar and run, distance and sprints. Then we'd hit the bag, and do push-ups and sit-ups, and hit the bag again. But it had been four years since his last bout, and Van, at thirty-nine, was nearing the end of his boxing career.

At the end of each workout, he'd light up a smoke. The first time I saw this, I stared in horror. "Van the Man," I exclaimed. "You, you know you can't do that."

Van took a deep breath. "I know, I know, but brother, I can't stop." So the clogging of his lungs continued to the night of the fight.

During the first round Van came out quickly, bobbing and weaving, moving forward, and throwing hard punches. He was rocking his much younger opponent, a rangy white guy who, as I remember, spent three minutes on his heels, unable to get off a shot.

The Sahib of old? A first round knockout? I hoped so. But the clang of the bell saved Tim and doomed Van.

During the second round, Van came out slower. He was breathing hard and started taking punches from his rejuvenated foe. He wasn't fighting back.

I closed my eyes. The end, I knew, was near.

I don't remember if the knockout came in that round or the following, but I do remember this: Van, hands at his sides, falling face first to the canvas. I would learn later that the fall or the punch that caused it took out three of his upper front teeth.

The crowd stood and cheered. "The white guy won, the white guy won," I imagined them thinking. I got up, walked out, and got in my car.

No radio. Just silence on the long drive home.

Van died in 2015. Over the years he and I and Teddy and the guys he trained stayed close. My friend Jimmy, who owned a gym in Seattle, joined this tight-knit group. Van would often stop by to work with Jimmy's fighters.

Several times a year, we'd meet and share a meal, laugh and drink, and tell stories. Sometimes he'd call just to touch base. Sometimes he'd call to tell us his problems—just lost a job, ran out of money, got arrested and dumped in jail—and we'd help if we could.

Van was estranged from his family. In thirty-six years of knowing him, I'd never met a single blood relative. For him, near the end it came down to Teddy, Jimmy, and me—the only family he had.

The last years of Van's life weren't easy. For too long, he'd lived in a raggedy house in South Seattle. Worse, he was a hoarder who'd collected old newspapers, magazines, zipperless jackets, old vases, broken televisions and radios. When I would visit, I'd have to pick my way to the kitchen table along a narrow trail through a thick dusty forest of useless things. The table was where he hosted guests.

One Sunday on a whim, I drove up from Tacoma to visit with Van. We sat at the kitchen table. It had been a few months since I'd seen him, and I was saddened and surprised. He'd lost weight. He walked with a cane and breathed through an inhaler hooked up to an oxygen tank.

On the table were an ashtray full of butts, a book of matches, and half a pack of smokes.

"Doc says I got CO somethin', somethin'."

"COPD," I said. "Means you got a problem with your lungs."

Jimmy Gilmore and Van Taylor, circa 2005. Photo courtesy of Jimmy Gilmore.

Van nodded. "Yeah, somethin' like that."

"And this," I said, pointing to the cigarettes, "this sure ain't helpin'." I stared at him. "You still got time, brother, save your lungs, or what's left of 'em. This ain't no joke. But you gotta help yourself."

"What you mean?"

I reached into my jacket pocket and pulled out a box of antismoking gum that I'd always carried with me. For a while, I'd taken up smoking, but I wanted to stop.

"Take these, man, it'll cut the craving," I said. I stood to leave and reached across the table, my hand hovering over the cigarettes. "You want me to take this?"

Van stared at me. "Nah, nah, man, I'll chew the gum. I'll be cool."

As I walked to my car, I felt uneasy. Van chewing the gum? Van being cool? I had my doubts. That afternoon, disturbed by Van's condition, I called Teddy.

"Been to see Van, and man, he's on oxygen but won't quit smokin'," I said. "Then there's all that clutter, all that damn dust." I stared at the wall. "Man, his place, it's just toxic."

"Yeah, I know. Been over there myself."

"You know he's on oxygen?"

"Nope, he never told me."

"Me neither," I said.

"I left him some nicotine gum, but you know Van."

"Yup. It's still where you left it."

I took a deep breath and exhaled. "Teddy, we gotta do something. Maybe move him out . . . somethin'."

"I know," he said. "I'll get back to you."

A month later, Teddy called me back. He'd found out through a contact in city government that there was a subsidized unit in a new elderly complex off Rainier Avenue. It was close to Chubby & Tubby and not too far from where Van was living. A grocery store was nearby. Perfect.

Teddy gave Van the application papers for him to fill out and sign. At first, Van was stubborn, hesitant; he didn't want to move. So much of his life was tied up in there. But his opinion changed when his landlord notified him that he was selling the house Van was living in.

Teddy took the papers and delivered them to the complex manager. A week or so later, he got word that Van had been approved. Now all that was left was to physically move him. And that was a job I'll never forget. The three of us— Teddy, Jimmy, and I—agreed to meet at Van's place, 8:00 sharp, on the last Saturday of July. His lease at the new unit would start the first of August.

That Saturday happened to be the hottest day of the summer, and since it was near the first of the month, renting a big truck proved to be very costly. It's called gouging.

Credit cards, I sighed, as I signed my name to an unplanned $500 bill. It's why God created them.

For the first four hours, Jimmy, Teddy, and I worked nonstop. Teddy left at noon, pleading a prior engagement. He was the smart one. All the while Van was standing to the side and pointing with his cane, directing the action and telling us what we had to take.

"Oh, and hey," Van said, "don't forget this record player, and this here toaster, and oh, oh, don't forget this rockin' chair."

After an hour, I was exhausted, drenched in sweat. "But Van, they're broken," I protested.

"You can put 'em in storage," he said. "They valuable, man, they like antiques, and I'll get around to gettin' 'em fixed."

Storage, a side trip and another cost I hadn't thought of. So three hundred credit card bucks later, Van had his storage unit. By the end of the day, Jimmy and I were exhausted, barely standing. But Van the Man had his apartment.

When I got home, I was ten pounds lighter. Every muscle in my body ached, like I'd just gone three hard rounds against someone good.

"How was it?" my wife Mary asked.

I shook my head. "Offa this?" I said, and laughed. "After today, honey, Jimmy, Teddy, and me, we goin' to heaven. Straight up, no pause, not a minute in purgatory, no doubt about that."

✦

The apartment is where Van lived his last few years. Jimmy, Teddy, and I would call him and invite him out. Teddy or Jimmy would pick him up and we'd meet in Chinatown for barbecue ribs and Chinese greens and Chinese beer. But for Van, going out got harder. So we adapted, calling him and visiting and bringing him chicken wings, ribs, white rice, and a favorite pint or fifth.

In his apartment on Sunday afternoons, we'd gather to eat and drink, laugh and tell stories. It was just like it had always been, but not quite.

Van was shrinking, having a hard time walking, having a harder time breathing. Then there were the increasingly frequent ER trips to the hospital where we'd gather and visit.

But he'd always return home. Until one day he didn't.

✦

A few weeks ago, Teddy sent me an email. Just touching base in the pandemic, the safest way imaginable.

"One more thing," he wrote. "I miss Van."

"I miss him, too," I wrote back.

Van the Man, I thought sadly. That dang old cranky dog. Man, he don't listen no how.

ONE OCTOBER DAY

On a long ago October afternoon, I picked up the phone and called my mother. "Mom," I said calmly. "I passed the bar."

She gasped. I could hear her cry. "Thank you," she said softly. "Thank you."

That's all she said. This though is what she meant.

Thank you, the oldest of my children.

On the day you were born I counted ten fingers, ten toes. You had brown wavy hair. What was not for me to love.

Thank you as well for not complaining. For being the easiest baby to raise. You didn't even scream when I changed your diapers and I, being new to this, would accidently prick you. You would furrow your brow and look concerned, but never did you cry or complain or condemn me for carelessness or bad motherhood.

I knew right then you weren't the complaining type.

As a young child, you ate fig bars and cold Spam sandwiches on Wonder Bread. You drank powdered milk—and Tang, just like an astronaut.

I'm sure many of your friends ate better, especially those with brick homes close to the lake. But you didn't complain because you knew even then that was all we could afford. Then through the grace of Jesus who died for our sins and Dad finding steady work, we scraped up enough for piano lessons, and I thought, "That's what you'll do." And you played because you loved me. I know that. You hated it and didn't like your teacher; I knew that, too.

Your passions were baseball and basketball. But you stayed with it for seven years because you knew how I wished I could have played—impossible because we were always on the move, always hiding from those bad, bad Japanese.

Then one day, you'd just turned thirteen, I think, you told me no more piano. You'd had enough. By then you were old enough to start to know your mind.

"Okay," I said.

Was I disappointed? A little. I thought to myself, "No concerts. No sold-out halls. No junior Liberace. No television shows." I sighed. "But at least I've got a good son."

And now you're an attorney. How 'bout dat?

And your office, son, your father and I, Uncle Vic and Uncle Rico, we can't wait to visit. Can we? Will you have a window and a view of the bay and the mountains?

What about photos. I will take them? Would you mind? Of course not.

Hoy, a haircut. Now you need one. You really do. Also a new suit. No more jeans and T-shirts for you, Misturrr. Meet me tomorrow, Nordstrom's.

Oh, and thank you for the grandchildren you'll bring me.
At least three, right? They will look like you and your Vivian—
a beautiful girl from a good Filipino family.

Jesus, Maria, Josep, Peter. My prayers have been
answered. You've made this the happiest day of my life.

But I know there'll be other joys to follow. I know that,
and I can hardly wait.

✦

Mom, your joys would have to wait. For you, especially, I know that my immediate post–law school years must have been hard. My marriage, the first one, was falling apart because of my immaturity, my rampant infidelity. Then I stopped being an attorney and, far worse, not a grandchild in sight.

One afternoon, you, in a rare fit of pique, shook your head and said, "Son, you're such a disappointment."

And I was—to her, to myself. But hearing Mom say it hit me hard. I stopped calling. I stopped visiting. I was embarrassed. Two weeks later, she called me.

"Why have you stopped calling?"

"You said I was a disappointment."

"Oh, you're not anymore."

And just like that, we're good again. And that's how we were for almost seventy years. Mother and I, a teaspoonful of words, our bond unbreakable.

Your joys would eventually come. Like in the early 1980s, when I started writing and getting published. First, on the editorial pages of the Seattle papers, then regional and national publications. My message was the same: that Philippine dictator Ferdinand Marcos was bad, not just for Filipinos but for America.

But Marcos was Washington's boy. He crooned anti-Communist lyrics and pledged that vital US bases could stay forever and a day in his archipelago—for a price, of course, paid to him. No questions asked. No answers expected.

My work was getting noticed. Even in Seattle, older Filipinos were starting to talk. One friend warned Mom that the Philippine Consulate was keeping an eye on me; I was on a list, which made sense because Marcos was a highly paid American puppet. Public criticism and erosion of US support threatened him, his family, and the millions he'd managed to steal in US aid.

"Be careful," Mom whispered to me. And although she looked worried, I knew she was proud. Her oldest child, an enemy of the state. How 'bout dat?

Despite the warning, conveyed in the fall, I returned to the Philippines in November 1983, just before Thanksgiving break at the University of Washington. I was teaching a class on Philippine history, and Manila, as usual, was floating in rumors.

Ferdinand Marcos had disappeared from public view for several days, and the rumors ran the gamut.

"Hoy, a friend of my cousin whose auntie works in the palace said he's gravely ill."
"My guess, kumpadre, he's already dead."
"Who'll take his place?"
"What about the generals?"
"Maybe they're already running things."
"What about the Communists? The Muslims?"
"Will there be a civil war?"
"Will the Americans get involved?"

I felt like a fraud, a reclining-chair journalist. A huge story in the Marcos era, and I wasn't there. It had been three years since I once followed an old lover into the jungle. It was time to return.

After class, I booked a flight for Manila. Two days later, I was gone.

Now, in making this decision I hadn't entirely lost my mind. In 1983 I could enter the Philippines on my US passport—no visa necessary, no heads up to consular officials keeping an eye on me. Plus there was this intangible that I had considered. Consular officials I'd met didn't strike me as especially smart, competent, or disciplined—a trait that I believed (and hoped) ran through the entire repressive Marcos machine.

And sure enough, when I was clearing customs at Manila International, a soldier in a booth nodded at me. He lit up a smoke, then continued reading his newspaper. The computer on his desk was turned off.

The next three days turned out to be a major waste of time and money. Marcos was sick but not dead. There would be no major story breaking out of Manila.

When I returned to Seattle, I drove to my parents' house to wish them belated Thanksgiving greetings.

"Hi Mom," I said cheerily.

"Hi son, where have you been?" She kissed me on the cheek.

"Ooh, I just got back from Manila."

She gasped and rolled her eyes. "You're a bad, bad boy," Mom said, but she was smiling when she said it. She then turned toward the kitchen. "You should eat."

✦

When Marcos died, he took my journalism career with him. With the world watching, he would strut and preen like the vilest WWE heel. But now that show was over; the international journalists had gathered their pens and notes and gone home.

And that was fine with me. By then I'd turned my attention to fiction. My goal: to write my first novel. Over the years I had wondered why so many journalists found fiction so alluring, and I think I have the answer, or at least my answer.

As reporters and editorial writers, we start with facts and go from there. But I began to wonder: What if I created my own facts, my own world, and sprinkled it with characters born and raised in my imagination? I would see their faces and hear their words. I would feel to my core their fears, sorrows, and joys. I would talk to them, and they'd talk back.

Then I would put them in conflict. I would determine the outcome. I would decide who would live and die. Kind of like God. And creating a fictional universe will be the closest I will ever come to divinity.

Writing a novel is a yearslong wrestling match full of weaknesses, wrong moves, and nagging doubts. Does the scene work? How about this word, keep it? Change it? Does the narrative have a rhythm? Will it rise to the level of art?

In 1989 I submitted my first novel, *CEBU*, to the University of Washington Press, which had published a well-regarded line of Asian American fiction. The next year, the UW Press notified me that my novel was accepted—release date 1991.

The initial reviews were mixed, but in 1992 *CEBU* won an American Book Award. At the time, I was living in San Francisco and scheduled to do a lecture in Virginia Beach, so I asked Mom and Dad to attend the awards ceremony in my place. I called my mom after I returned to San Francisco.

"How was it?"

"Your father," she said. "He was going around to the different tables, carrying your book, pointing to your picture on the back. I think he was bothering people, you know how he is, but I finally got him to sit down and eat."

Mom said that Dad had been going to the UW Press office to ask for books to sell. Then he'd go down to Chinatown and sell them to his pals, even those who couldn't read.

In 1993, before he died, Mom called to ask me to talk to Dad. They had been to yet another funeral, another old Pinoy gone. Our community was disappearing. But Dad was unfazed by the deaths of old friends. At the funeral mass he'd brought several copies of *CEBU* with him.

"At the cemetery, your father was selling your book to the mourners, the widow, even to the priest." She paused. "I was so embarrassed. Please talk to him."

I giggled.

"It's not funny."

"Yes, it is."

"Funny to you, maybe, but I have to live here," she said and then sighed. "When you stopped being an attorney, it broke his heart. He didn't say so, I know he didn't talk to you, but I knew. Your father's not much for words, least not American words. And now this, his son, the award-winning author, better than being a lawyer."

I was quiet for a moment, maybe even a little longer. In my mind, a collage of scenes: of Dad nodding when I hit a jump shot, of Dad smiling at my law school graduation, of him crying at my wedding.

"Hoy, Peter."

"Um, sorry Mom."

"It's just his way of showing how proud he is of you."

I took a deep breath. Composed myself. "How 'bout dat," I softly said.

ARNAUD

More than forty years ago, the late Arnaud de Borchgrave changed my life.

In the mid-1970s he was everything I wasn't:
urbane, insightful, audacious, and brave. When he was
writing for *Newsweek*, I'd go straight to his dispatches written after he'd hopped a plane to cover this or that Third
World battle or to interview this or that big man of the
moment. This entire troubled world was his beat.

I wasn't Arnaud, but I wasn't doing badly. In fact, by
most measures I was doing very well. I was a new attorney
employed by the City of Seattle and married to a lovely and
wonderful woman, my first wife Vivian. My immigrant parents, for whom hardship, poverty, and racism had been the
norm, were giddily proud.

When I passed the bar, I called Mom to tell her the news.
I could hear her softly crying. Then she gathered herself.

"Thank you," she finally whispered. Could children, an office with a view, a six-figure salary, and a house in a nice neighborhood be far behind?

On the surface my life was perfect. But the problem was I couldn't get de Borchgrave out of my mind. And the longer he stayed, the more clearly I realized that the life I was living—my marriage, my first profession, my parents' immigrant dreams—would soon be over.

So, in 1976, I stopped being an attorney and fortunately landed on my feet at the University of Washington, where I taught undergraduates the basics of law, legal history, and any other course that caught my eye. It turned out I had a knack for teaching, and I'm still doing what I did as a much younger man.

A few years later, I stopped being a husband.

Our marriage was a death by slicing, with me wielding the knife. First came the times apart—my insistence that even in marriage we were independent beings and my belief that monogamy was an obsolescent 1950s relic, followed by the overlong stays at the office, the times apart, and then the affairs themselves.

Explore and enjoy the boundaries, I told myself at the time, push them back. The center will hold. And, of course, it did not.

In retrospect, it is a wonder that Vivian and I lasted until 1980, a few months after I'd returned from the dangerous Philippine island of Samar and the last tortured moments with Mae, an old lover. We were idiots trying to be journalists in a land that killed both.

"Peter," Vivian said. "Our marriage is over."

I gulped. But even then, I couldn't blame her. She should have left sooner.

Would I miss her? Yes, and deeply. Did I deserve her? Absolutely not.

Our time together—my unbounded foolishness—gnawed at my heart. Years into my second marriage, I dreamed of Vivian and woke up crying. My wife was sleeping, a tiny mercy.

But the remains of a failed marriage can sometimes unleash new energies. And for me that meant writing—getting published, seeing my byline, getting paid. When Vivian and I were married, I'd talked about it enough—that writing about exciting, important things was what I really wanted to do.

"So write," Vivian said.

But I never did. Maybe it was the security and comfort, the predictability of marriage. No need to stretch; life will go on. Or maybe it was my fear that as a writer I wouldn't be good enough.

When Vivian left, she took away the former and left me with the latter. It was time to either become a writer or admit it was a fantasy, an ego-driven phantasm that only fools believed.

I decided then I would write about the Philippines—a violent and very dangerous place full of insurgencies, skeletal brown children with red hair and distended stomachs, military assassinations, other random killings, and an aging, ailing, increasingly unpopular dictator whose soldiers killed his political rival. Toss in an extensive US military presence and the fact that the strongman, Ferdinand Marcos, assured the bases' ongoing presence (as long as the United States continued to pay him), and what you had was a recipe for chaos.

The Philippines in the 1980s was a screwed-up country on the cusp of revolution, a failing Third World state de Borchgrave would have loved.

And that's what I wanted to write about. That's where I wanted to be.

ANUGON

---

once followed a lover into the jungle.

Where: The city of Catbalogan, island of Samar,
Central Philippines.
When: 1980.
Why: To report on fighting between the Philippine
military and Communist insurgents.

In a long life filled with the detritus of stupid decisions,
this by far was the stupidest.

Actually, the "why" part is incomplete. I was also trying
to revive a dying romance with Mae, the lover in question,
who objected to me being married. Over time she became
increasingly angry, increasingly bitter. I should have walked
away, but I was hooked through my neck by this long-limbed,
high-cheekboned Eurasian beauty. Mine was a story as old
as the first erection.

"You asshole," she'd typically begin before continuing to my latest and growing litany of faults. "You just don't understand . . ."

I did understand, but what could I say? Free love, alternative lifestyles, question authority, John F. Kennedy, and other claptrap from the 1960s? For many baby boomers, it was selfishness masquerading as freedom and idealism. No wonder we folded when Trump and his jackals came. We weren't real to start with.

During Mae's tirades, I'd just shrug, shut up, and let her vent, hoping she'd change her mind, like Saul on the road to Damascus. But that had only happened once, once upon a time and a long time ago.

Other than getting rid of me, she said in a rare and temporary moment of calm, her goal was to become a foreign correspondent and to visit strange and dangerous places—to see her byline in national magazines and, fingers crossed, maybe even be on national TV.

"Like Geraldo Rivera," she added. I nodded solemnly and tried to picture lovely Mae with a mustache.

I sensed an opening. "Sure, why not?"

She arched an eyebrow—skeptical, suspicious, ready to pounce.

"And . . ."

I had a friend in Cebu, I explained. Dio was a dangerous man, an *escrimador*—a stick fighter of some renown. He knew violence. He knew what was going on. My bad-to-the-bone pal would guide us to where we needed to go.

For a moment, Mae's face softened. "But I can't afford it."

Another opening. "I can," I said.

"You're still an asshole."

And that's how we ended up in Catbalogan aboard a crowded jeepney heading east, across the hills, destination Taft, a small seaside town named after William Howard Taft, the corpulent former governor general of the colonial Philippines, who later went on to become president of the United States and, later, a Supreme Court justice.

At the town's edge, we passed two young men, Americans, walking out of the jungle. They were dressed in white shirts and black pants and shoes. The morning was unbearably muggy, as it always is, and this pair of displaced strollers didn't look happy.

"Mormons," I whispered to my companions, then turned toward the missionaries.

"Hi Joe," I said with a cheerful wave.

They looked at me, snarling. "Fuck you," they must have thought but, as Mormons, didn't dare say.

Over the next three, maybe four hours, the jeepney chugged along, eventually leaving the jungle floor and climbing into the hills. The change in elevation brought cooler air, which triggered relief and renewed conversation.

"My friends say the guerrillas are active in and around Taft," Dio said. "You'll find your story there."

I gulped and said nothing. For the first time, I thought that maybe this was a story that shouldn't be told—at least not by Mae and me. We were less than rookies, wannabe journalists who hadn't arranged beforehand what any real journalist would have—contacts, a guarantee of protection, an escape plan. I took a deep breath. It was too late now.

The jeepney began its descent, and a mile or so away and across a river lay Taft. We crossed a bridge over the river. I glanced down and blinked. Its color was black.

Once in Taft, we got out and sank into ankle-deep mud, which didn't hinder a marching band playing a forgettable tune, or a squad of soldiers on patrol. We learned from one of the locals that the town was celebrating the feast day of its patron saint, whoever that was.

The scene was ominous and surreal, hard to imagine, not of this world. Mae and I looked at each other. We looked at Dio. I wasn't the only one who felt this way.

"What should we do?" Mae asked.

I pointed to a nearby steeple. "A Catholic church," I said, summoning the remnants of my former faith and trying my best to sound confident. "We should go there."

I walked up the rectory steps and knocked on the door. A Filipino priest, short and plump, answered.

"Father," I began, "we're not from here . . ."

"No," he said and closed the door.

I motioned for Mae to join me. "Your turn," I said. "Seduce him with your eyes, smile, wiggle your butt, I don't care. Just get the dude to change his mind."

I walked down the steps and joined Dio. The door opened. We couldn't hear what Mae was saying, but she was smiling when she turned around.

"We can stay there," she said, "there" being an open-air shed on the edge of the parish grounds.

As we bedded down on the concrete floor, curious locals started coming around. One of them, Ting, was a young woman dressed in blue overalls. She smiled at Mae and sat beside her.

"Ah, journalists," Ting said.

"How do you know?" I asked.

She laughed. "Who else would come to this dangerous miserable edge of nowhere."

Ting lit a smoke and turned toward Mae. "You crossed our river. It's black, no? The copper mine upriver dumps its waste directly into the water, making us even poorer. But that's how it is here. The rich screw us. The Philippine Constabulary kills us when we complain. But that's life in Taft, on Samar, in most of the Philippines."

She took a deep breath and exhaled. "But never mind the river," she began. "I know why you're here. You want to know about the fighting, the disappearances, the murders, the guerrillas. No action today, though. It's a fiesta, so the fighting stops at least for today. But if you stay around I can—"

"No," I said. "We're going back first thing tomorrow." I looked first at Mae then Dio. No disagreement.

Ting frowned. "If you change your mind . . ."

"We won't," I said.

Across the street was a basketball court on which a makeshift stage had been built. A band started to play, and Taft's residents began to gather, then to dance. I watched as the court filled up with more dancers and others just nodding their heads to the beat. Their joy seemed desperate and real, not faked, and why not. A fiesta: No killing today.

A young soldier walked toward our shed. "The colonel," he announced, "would like the honor of a dance with the young lady, our guest for the evening."

Mae looked at me. I nodded. "Go," I said.

Mae shrugged, but before she turned to go, I walked over and grabbed her arm. "Dance your ass off," I whispered fiercely.

She walked toward the basketball court. The music stopped. The crowd parted as the colonel came forward to take Mae's hand and lead her to the dance floor. Then the music resumed and the dancers began stepping, churning, twirling, dipping.

I lost sight of Mae. But in my mind, I could see her moving to the beat—a thrust here, a wiggle there—each move elegant, every move seductive. She'd danced that way for me.

I sat down and a Bisayan word, *anugon*, came to mind. It connects two English words, "shame" and "waste," as in it would be such a shame to waste this foolish but beautiful foreigner. I believe to this day that this is what the colonel was thinking as he danced with his belle of the ball.

An hour or so later, Mae, face glistening, returned to the shed. I was on my side trying to sleep.

"So," she said. "What do you think?"

I turned to face her. "I think he'll let us leave."

And that's what happened. We boarded the outgoing jeepney the next morning with not a soldier in sight. We'd reach Catbalogan, then Cebu City. After that, we'd fly to Manila, then home.

Mae and I? I knew it was over. She did, too. Samar was a change in scene, not a change in facts. I was still married. She and I could go no further. Besides, she'd taken a liking to Dio.

Relief, that's what I felt. We could now at least move on.

In Manila, while awaiting my flight, a newspaper headline caught my eye: "Samar Bishop Asks for Investigation." On the basketball court in Taft the bodies of three young men had been dumped. My heart started racing. I took a deep breath.

So this is what it all boiled down to, the difference between living and dying: For the colonel, killing Mae would have been anugon.

And the three dead men? Not anugon enough.

JUST BEFORE NOON

"Just before noon on Aug. 28, I was returning from Quezon City, north of Manila. About 2 kilometers from Camp Aguinaldo I saw a column of [armored] personnel carriers moving toward Channel 4, the government television station. The station is in a walled compound, and earlier that morning it had been seized by a small rebel force.

"I followed the convoy and when it reached the rear staging area, a large crowd of civilians started to cheer. It was clear that the impasse would soon be broken. After parking the car, I ran after the column and watched the last vehicle enter the unguarded rear gate. At that time, I was perhaps 15 meters (50 feet) from the entrance and, as the last armored carrier disappeared into the compound, there was a large explosion, followed by bursts of automatic weapons fire.

"I dived to the ground but kept my head up to assess the situation, which included my own safety. Initially I was content *to stay prone but soon changed my mind. Across the street, a squad of attacking soldiers had assumed their positions, and their fire would soon be coming in my direction.*

"I crossed the street and sought cover behind a car parked in front of the Joint US Military Assistance Group building. I was about 20 meters from the wall and parallel with the squad's line of fire. Ten meters away, a two-man bazooka team was firing rounds at unseen foes behind the thick concrete wall.

"At that point, a large part of Friday's most important question had been answered: Government forces were attacking their rebel comrades, albeit from a distance. Would they now move forward?

"The squad did not do so immediately, but eventually the soldiers did, alone and in pairs. At that point, and although hard fighting remained, particularly at Camp Aguinaldo, the rebellion had failed. It was about 1:30 p.m. when I left the area."

—From "Manila: President Aquino digs in . . . ,"
Christian Science Monitor, September 17, 1987

E very story has an untold backstory. Sometimes the backstory is more interesting than what makes it onto the page. This may be the case here.

✦

The main show of August 28 had an opening act. The day before, I had interviewed Rodolfo Canieso. I was told he was the head of military intelligence. The new president, Corazon Aquino, had a rocky relationship with the military, which her predecessor, the dictator Ferdinand Marcos, used to keep himself in power. Soldiers grumbled about low pay and her lenience toward Communist rebels. Others plotted coups and took over buildings—minor flareups, really, and easily defused.

But the threat of something bigger, more dangerous worried me.

No problem, Canieso said. "The army is loyal."

Deception or incompetence? To this day I have no answer.

I returned to my hotel and had a drink. Soothed by Canieso's assurance, I slept well. I shouldn't have.

It was late afternoon and just hours away from "something bigger, more dangerous" touching down in Manila. Just after midnight on the 28th, trucks and buses full of heavily armed soldiers rolled into Manila. Their goal: to capture or kill Corazon Aquino.

And they came damn close.

The first target was Malacanang Palace, the president's official residence. This band of about fifty rebels was met by Aquino's security detail who engaged them in an intense and deadly firefight involving automatic weapons, grenades, and mortars. After an hour or so, the mutineers withdrew. For the moment, at least, the president was safe.

Not so lucky was Aquino's son, "Noynoy," caught in a car near the palace when the battle erupted. The rebels killed three of his four bodyguards, and the son was hit in his neck and shoulder. His wounds were very serious, and in those early morning hours with everything in doubt, his mother faced a bitter, heart-wounding irony.

Just four years before, her husband, opposition leader Benigno Aquino, had been murdered by a Marcos goon. She'd buried her husband. Would she now bury her son?

Friday morning, I awoke to a city under siege. The head of hotel security, a former air force colonel, said that hundreds of rebels had fanned out and seized key sites, including Camp Aguinaldo and Channel 4.

"Damn," I grumbled. "I just slept through the year's biggest story out of Asia."

My disappointment was fueled by my realization that the titanic Aquino-Marcos struggle, with its overarching theme of good versus evil, had caught and had held the world's attention. Now, with Marcos in exile and Aquino in power, Manila was again a news backwater. Most of the foreign press had gone home.

The story of the attempted coup—this story—it should have been mine.

Later that morning I took a calculated risk. I would head north and leave Manila to do a prearranged interview with Luis Taruc, the legendary peasant guerrilla leader of decades past. Taruc had views on Aquino and the Communist insurgency. I wanted to hear them. Besides, the city was quiet now and negotiations were undoubtedly under way. Maybe the mutiny would be resolved without drama and further bloodshed.

If so, no front-page story there.

And besides, Taruc was several pages of twentieth-century Philippine history, a living symbol of ongoing peasant resistance in the Philippines' feudal and impoverished countryside, where big landlords exploited their tenants and landless laborers. The rural Philippines had been a powder keg since the 1930s. In the five decades since, not much had changed. A new generation of desperate peasants was now picking up the gun and becoming foot soldiers for the Marxist New People's Army, yet one more threat to President Aquino.

✦

The interview with Luis Taruc went well. He was lean and spry, wearing his seventy-four years well. I was in awe, but he was also gracious and honest and put me at ease. When I asked him about Aquino, he said that he liked her. She was a good person—decent but not aggressive enough in pushing much needed reforms.

"Like what?" I asked.

"Land reform, break up the haciendas," Taruc answered. "If peasants get land, they'll put down their guns and come out of the hills."

"Just like that?"

He nodded. "Just like that."

✦

Just like that, I thought, on the ride back to Manila. And, of course, I knew it wasn't that easy. Over the years I had immersed myself in the Philippines and knew too well its tortured history.

The irony of Philippine democracy is that it gives the democratically elected elites a chance to beat back any measure that threatens their power and wealth. And with Congress reconvened, that was precisely what was happening. I lit a cigarette and sighed. The Philippines would remain a perpetual ER case: cyanotic blue, just minutes from the end.

And my written words of warning? Faint whispers in the wind.

"Just before noon on Aug. 28, I was returning from Quezon City, north of Manila. About 2 kilometers from Camp Aguinaldo I saw a column of [armored] personnel carriers moving toward Channel 4, the government television station."

I jabbed my driver in the arm and pointed excitedly. "Follow those armored personnel carriers!" I screamed, knowing full well this would be the first and last time I'd ever say what I just said.

"I followed the convoy and when it reached the rear staging area, a large crowd of civilians started to cheer. It was clear the impasse would soon be broken . . . I ran after the column . . ."

The street in the rear staging area was perpendicular to a corner of the wall surrounding Channel 4. That afternoon, hundreds of residents came out to cheer the convoy. I was running as hard as I could, but then the armored personnel carriers turned left, parallel with the wall, and I followed, still running. As I turned the corner, I suddenly realized that I was alone.

Alone.

It is a feeling that, even now, is hard to describe. At that moment I was hearing nothing. Not the cheering of the crowd, not the rumble of the APCs, not even the cicadas.

Nothing.

But I didn't turn around and say, "Oops, I've just made a horrible mistake." I never stopped. Instead I ran harder like the teenage jock I used to be.

What propelled me wasn't bravery. I had done my level best to live an unbrave life. The red badge of courage? No thanks. I'll pass. Give it to Ted Divina, Norm Dumlao, Larry Alcantara, and my other Pinoy brothers who were brave on a regular basis in the swamps of Vietnam.

What kept me going was ego. That's all it was—the chance to witness an important story, write about it, and call it my own.

"As the last armored carrier disappeared into the compound, there was a large explosion, followed by bursts of automatic weapons fire. I dived to the ground but kept my head up to assess the situation, which included my own safety. Across the street, a squad of attacking soldiers had assumed their position, and their fire would soon be coming in my direction."

After the explosion, dozens of Filipino civilians ran out of the compound. One of them, a thin young man, joined me on the ground. We were nose to nose, not six inches apart. For whatever reason, I was calm, out-of-body calm, and wondering if I should inch forward and enter the compound for a ringside seat.

But first, I needed a smoke. I checked my pockets.

Damn, no matches.

So I asked my new companion, "Hey, man, you got a light?" He looked at me like I'd lost my mind. He nodded to a street almost perpendicular to the compound gate. Not fifty yards away, a two-man bazooka team was getting ready to fire over us.

"Boss, we better get out of here," my companion said.

I nodded. "Yeah, I think you're right."

I sprang to my feet and ran low and hard, zigging and zagging as I went. I slid head first behind the rear wheel of a car and watched the bazooka team fire round after round over the wall. Eventually, other soldiers began to move forward. At that point, I knew the mutiny had failed.

✦

By late afternoon, I was standing on the roof of my hotel scanning the vast panorama of Manila. Black smoke billowed along the city's northern edge. In the distance a World War II vintage warplane dove toward its target. I turned away. I had had enough.

The city had not seen such devastation since 1945, when American and Filipino forces rooted out the Japanese. The fighting was fierce. In the end the Allies won, but Manila lost—many of its neighborhoods and much of its downtown reduced to rubble.

And now this. *Sad*, I thought, the saddest thing I'd ever seen. So tragic and absurd. So futile. So stupid.

Arnaud de Borchgrave would have loved the violence and chaos.

Me, not so much. I'd just spent ninety minutes in a firefight. That was enough for my lifetime—not one minute more. I promised myself then I would never return to this troubled, dangerous, ungovernable land that my parents had left decades ago.

This promise I have kept.

OTHER REASONS TO STAY HOME

- In 1992 Aquino's successor, Fidel Ramos, granted amnesty to the leader of the mutiny, Colonel Gregorio Honasan.

- In 1995 Filipino voters elected Honasan to the Philippine Senate. He was reelected in 2001.

- As of 1995 no one killed during the 1987 mutiny has risen from the dead.

- In the 2016 presidential race, Filipino voters chose Rodrigo Duterte, whose penchant for killing criminal suspects is well established and well known.

- In 2017 a Pew Research Center poll found that Donald Trump's "greatest support . . . comes from Filipinos, 69 percent of whom say they have confidence in the US president."

A NOTE ON BIENVENIDO SANTOS

I owe a lot to the late Filipino writer Bienvenido Santos.

For starters, Santos, in his brilliant and evocative collection, *Scent of Apples*, showed me the beauty of the short story format, the masterful use of subtlety in both narrative and dialogue, and the proper linkage of related stories that in this case created an elegant work of art as satisfying as any well-crafted novel.

But there's another, more personal reason as well.

As a Pinoy, an American-born son raised on the "manong" stories of my pioneering father and uncles, I had thought that all Pinoys were poor—surely, the ones I knew were. I also thought that Filipino America in the 1940s was geographically limited to the West Coast, with Stockton and Seattle as the epicenters of Filipino American life. I am thankful that more than three decades ago, Santos showed me I was wrong on both counts.

Although the first story, "Immigration Blues," is set in San Francisco while the last, "Footnote to a Laundry List," is set in Manila, these are essentially bookends, well crafted, certainly, but not central to the heart of the collection, which begins with "Scent of Apples," featuring Santos as the narrator ("Ben"). He tells the stories of ordinary Filipinos such as the Michigan farmer Celestino Fabia in "Scent of Apples" and of his bitter soon-to-be drafted cousin Manuel in "And Beyond, More Walls."

But Santos also tells the stories of young Filipinos stranded in Washington, DC, during the war. Most of the young men and women are students at America's finest universities, sent there by their landed elite and very wealthy Filipino parents. Their goal is to get a degree from a famous US university—a "gold card" credential in the US-centric colonial Philippines. Their parents' expectation is that they then return, degree and new skills in hand, to help their families run their varied enterprises and (Santos was far too polite to say so, but I'm not) to exploit poor and desperate Filipinos.

This point does not escape Santos. Starting with "The Hurt Men," Santos introduces his readers to Val, Doc, and the other Filipino exiles gathered around a poker table in Washington, DC. Their banter is light, full of well-educated, socially proper bonhomie. Their academic pedigrees (Harvard, Columbia, the University of Chicago) and their wealth are obvious. These young men of privilege are different from their migrant, stoop-labor peers in California. Val, for example, has "a light complexion, lighter than any of ours, and arms as he rolled his sleeves, were plump and soft like a girl's."

But the men do hurt, and they hurt in different ways and to different degrees because of their separation from their homeland and the carnage, loss, and chaos unleashed by the war, including the wholesale devastation of Manila during the liberation. Readers are also introduced to Ambo, albeit indirectly. Val tells Ben near the end of the story, "You should meet Ambo."

There is no doubt that Ambo, whose real name is "Pablo," is the central character in the collection. In a later story, "Manila House," Val describes him as "a little elderly Filipino" who during the Great Depression "had a whole household of Filipinos feeding on everything he could give them. . . . He is well loved by the Filipino community."

High praise, indeed. But then Val adds this backhanded caveat: "If he had on.of our countrymen in this country."

In the reviews of this collection, much has been made of Santos's ability to capture the sense of displacement of Val and the other "hurt men," the *bayanihan* spirit, and so forth.

Little has been written about Santos's unerring ability to stab Filipino elites and their deep hypocrisies. In that sense, *Scent of Apples* is, at its core, subversive.

For example, as to Val's claims that these Filipinos "love" Ambo, the question arises as to whether that affection is genuine, or is it shallow and really based on need? Ambo takes care of them; he gets things done. In the Philippines, rich Filipinos have servants just like Ambo to cater to their every need. Not so in Washington during the war.

The question is answered in "Letter: The Faraway Summer," when Ambo/Pablo pays a visit to his old friend Doc, who has established a successful medical practice in Manila.

Ambo has returned to the Philippines, but now he has second thoughts. He wants Doc to use his American embassy connections to get a visa to return to America. Doc greets Ambo coolly and suggests that he write him a letter of introduction to the embassy. After brushing Ambo off, Doc dials his wife or lover—a conversation that Ambo overhears. Doc apologizes for being late, explaining that he was held up "by a man, a Pinoy . . . I said Pinoy, just one of those Pinoys I had met in the States . . ."

(In writing this line of dialogue denigrating Ambo, Santos has also created a teaching moment. Today the term *Pinoy* is loosely applied to all Filipinos. Appropriation, Filipino style, right? But for me, the term, as originally used, had geographic [America], ethnic [Filipino], and working-class connotations. It belonged to Ambo and to my father's and uncles' generation and to their American-born children. Ahistorical appropriation doesn't change it.)

In assembling this collection, it is clear that Santos's favored characters are Pinoys such as Ambo, Celestino Fabia, and Bernie Canlas in "The Contender." Bernie is an ex-fighter losing his eyesight; in his despair he apologizes to other Pinoys for never winning the championship.

Finally, there's Fil Canlas in "The Day the Dancers Came." This old Pinoy's only wish is to invite the young, pretty, and privileged dancers of a touring national troupe—undoubtedly the acclaimed Bayanihan Philippine National Folk Dance Company—to a homemade dinner in his rundown Chicago apartment. After the performance he approaches the dancers, but "they were always moving away."

Dejected, Fil returns home and describes his encounter to Tony, another old Pinoy and his roommate and friend. "They looked through me. I didn't exist. Or worse, I was unclean. *Basura*. Garbage. They were ashamed of me. How could I be Filipino?"

Less favored are characters like Doc and Val, who shows his true colors, his cowardice, his absolute lack of spine, in "Quicker with Arrows." In this fascinating story, Val has been dating Fay, a kind and loving working-class white woman. For Val the affair should stay a secret because his wealthy parents in the Philippines would disapprove of their son marrying beneath his station. The test comes when Val's elite Filipino friends come to visit.

Val's reaction? He asks Fay to stay in the bedroom.

For reviewers who are intimately familiar with the subject matter, there is a tendency to overly focus on political and social themes such as class, so prevalent in Philippine culture. And perhaps that has been the case here. But to focus mainly on this would be to sell Santos, the literary artist, short.

Santos is a short-form master, able to merge clear visual narrative with poetic sensibility. Nowhere is this more evident than in the closing paragraph of "Lonely in the Autumn Evening":

And when they buried Nanoy, the wind was blowing from the river across the hillock where a group of us stood bareheaded under a dark September sky. A wooden cross painted white, bore his name and the date of his passing. Nobody spoke and our heads were bowed in grief. I looked at the mud sticking to my shoes. It was reddish brown and soft, like earth on a hillock after the rain. I have seen such earth before, in the muddy fields among the Sinicaran hills in Albay, along the muddy trails in June beneath the church of

Antopolo. But as we walked away and I looked back, a dark smoke floated among the dying trees in the graveyard wind-borne from a dozen chimneys of a sprawling ammunitions factory. Nanoy's grave stood lonely in the autumn evening.

A CLOSE CALL, MEMORIES, A LAST GOODBYE

HEART ATTACK

March 27, 2019.

Dying is one thing—no big deal; everyone does it. But standing outside your body and watching yourself die—now that's something else. And it's exactly what I did on March 27, when my heart attack hit, and I watched my body crumble. I watched the doc work furiously, ignoring the different, grating flatline tones.

Then I notice for the first time my wife Mary, who was closing her eyes and praying to a god she'd too long ignored. I feel her love, her growing despair, her private and pending unwailed sorrow. For almost twenty years she has been the center of my life, and I desperately want us to go longer. Unlike the wives in my two earlier marriages, Mary became my sole focus. And along the way I came to appreciate her sensuality, her perceptive and skeptical intellect, her acute artistic insight, and her open and selfless heart.

What was not to love?

With her, I gave up my late-night meanderings. Gone as well were the strange, alien scents smothered by cigarette smoke. I did not miss any of it.

Mary is my focus, the one I hope to protect. And I can, but only if I can reenter my lifeless body which, somehow, I am able to do. I feel my eyes flutter, then open.

"What happened?" I manage to ask you.

"Heart attack, your entire system—heart, kidneys, lungs, name it—it all broke down, failed."

"But not enough," I say.

You shake your head. "No, not enough."

"Good," I say as I kiss your hand and close my eyes. "I think I'm gonna fart."

You roll your eyes. "Cheap trick."

Groggy, I still manage to smile and nod. "The best."

✦

In my dream of the day I died, Mary and I are driving along the Commencement Bay shoreline on our way to the hospital. Dawn has broken and we stop to watch the sun rise in the windless red and white sky over the Cascades. Farther south is the majesty of Mount Rainier, which has blessed us for centuries but could still kill us all.

I need this moment.

Visiting doctors makes me nervous. In the past I've postponed appointments or skipped them altogether. This time though you are adamant.

"X-rays, a black spot," you say. "Get it fixed."

I step out of the car to light a mix of tobacco and sage to bless Mary and me. I take a deep breath and think, the beauty of this place, it's the reason I came home. It's also a reason most never leave.

I return to the car and lean back. "How much time?"

"Half an hour, maybe more."

"Good," I say sleepily. "Take your time."

✦

But that's not how it happened.

After I'd vomited at home, you shoved me into the front seat of our Kia and drove like a madwoman east, toward the ER. We'd made it through the door just minutes before my life-and-death struggle began.

The great American writer Tim O'Brien claims there are two kinds of truth—"literal truth," in which Mary rushes me to the hospital and I somehow manage to survive, and "story truth," which may or may not have occurred as recounted on the page. Literal truth serves journalism, providing answers to who, what, when, and where. Whereas story truth serves a more demanding, creative master, providing insights to, say, the narrator's character and providing the slightest of hints that his death may be an event of surprising sorrow and power.

Our drive along Commencement Bay is story truth. In my retelling of this part of the story, this is the version I will use.

✦

I am now sitting up and chatting with Mary and two of my closest friends from the Seattle area, Jimmy Gilmore and Teddy Divina. I am fully conscious. The crisis is over.

Even on a good traffic day it is a challenge driving from Seattle to Tacoma, but here they are, their second visit in two days. I am touched, more than I show.

Our talk story runs the gamut, from Jimmy's daily challenge of raising a grandchild to Teddy's visit to the Ms' opening day in Tokyo. A raised eyebrow here, a soft chuckle there, nodded heads and rolled eyes, and an "Oh my, he didn't really do that, did he?" We're longtime friends—no need to say much.

What I really want to hear now is Teddy's laugh, which starts deep in his gut, drowns then swallows the punch line, and just keeps rolling.

I toss some bait. "Hey, man," I say. "Any word from your pal Randazzo?"

Over the years he'd talk about the legendary Teddy Randazzo, his teenage pre–Vietnam War Wapato alias. This was no ordinary change in names; it was a magical change in identities thorough enough to deceive most watchful fathers and brothers and suspicious, armed, and homicidal boyfriends.

I was skeptical at first. Randazzo's hair, combed back rather than parted at the side, didn't seem like much of a disguise, kind of like Clark Kent's glasses. But it seemed to work, and eventually I became convinced: On some level, Teddy Randazzo was real.

"There was this one time outside Wapato," Teddy began. "Me and this Yakama girl Eva and her whacked-out brother Joe, who'd promised to kill the legendary and elusive Randazzo, and . . ." Then he started laughing, a deep full laughter—a language of its own.

I'm not sure how the story ended, not that I care. I just wanted to hear him laugh. I think I'll even have him tape it. That way I can carry it with me and, before dying, hear it once again—a pet sound, familiar and soothing.

Like everyone else, I'll be waiting at this gate. But lucky me, I'll also have Mary's limitless love, a sunrise over the bay, Jimmy's enduring, good-natured patience, and Teddy's one-of-a-kind laugh, all remnants of a life I am about to leave.

A life of meaning, a good life overall.

MAP 7

n my dream the date is September 7, 2019.

I am at the Calvary Cemetery on 35th Avenue NE, standing inside the brick mausoleum in the northeast corner. A Filipino priest solemnly leads us in prayer and then addresses my family, other relatives, and close friends. At the end we inter my mother, who lies next to my father, who died in 1994.

My sister, a nephew, and my niece are crying. They are inconsolable. Others are crying, too. But I do not.

I do not because my mom's death was such a long-running affair, ever since the onset of senile dementia several years earlier. During that time as she began to enter her world of dreams and vivid memories I mourned because I knew how this would end. At the cemetery on that day in September, I have no tears left.

After I returned from California, I would drive up to visit her each Sunday, and we would sit and chat at the breakfast table. It was our wandering-son-returns-home ritual, one we both enjoyed. Over time what she would say—once so funny, wise, and focused—becomes increasingly incoherent. Over time her words change into fragments of thought trapped in a loop.

On one visit I bring her the *Seattle Times*. When she was younger, she loved reading the newspaper, especially the fat Sunday edition. She loved being informed. It is an attitude and a habit she's passed on to me.

I am thinking—and hoping—that maybe reading will engage her mind and strengthen her focus. We are sitting at the dining room table when I hand the front page to her. She smiles and thanks me. Then Mom starts reading, but after a few minutes she suddenly puts the paper down.

"You know, I still have property in Cebu," she says.

"I know, Mom," I say.

"I do, you know."

She resumes reading, turning pages and mumbling and nodding at news stories she likes while frowning and furrowing her brow at stories she doesn't. Mom adjusts her glasses and squints her eyes. She seems engaged, a good sign. I am hopeful, as I sit quietly, sipping coffee and nibbling a slice of toast.

After half an hour or so, she puts down the paper again and looks at me. I'm thinking that a story may have caught Mom's attention, perhaps bringing her joy or firing her indignation.

I smile. "Well, Mom," I begin. "So what's in the news?"

"I still have property in Cebu," she says.

✦

At the cemetery, I am praying for my mother, hoping that she is peaceful and well. I try my best to concentrate, but my mind wanders to the start of this year and the events that quickly follow.

In short order, the youngest son of close friends, a wonderful couple, unexpectedly dies. Then I come down with bronchitis, which I ignore.

"It's just a cold," I assure Mary. "I'll get through this like I've always done." For the past twenty years, I have rarely been sick. And on those rare days that I was, my body has always quickly bounced back. It was a point of pride, a foolish arrogance. Why should this be any different.

A few weeks later Mom is admitted to the ICU at Swedish Hospital in Seattle. Our family is on death watch. Mary and I drive to Seattle on a cold-to-the-bone, blustery day; we spend the night taking turns and staying by her bedside.

My bronchitis worsens, and although I don't realize it, it turns into pneumonia. I ignore that, too.

Somehow, Mom manages to cheat death. The doctors release her, and she returns to my sister Irma's house. I tell Mary I am driving to Seattle to say goodbye.

"You can't," she says. "Look at you. You're exhausted and sick. You need to go to the doctor."

"I've got to," I say. "I'll see the doc later."

When I arrive at Irma's house, Lio, Irma's husband, opens the door. Mom, wrapped in blankets, is sitting on a couch in the living room. Because of my fever, I stay on the porch and wave. Mom smiles and waves back. She recognizes me. It is a rare, precious moment of clarity, and I am glad.

"Peter, my son Peter?" she asks. "Hoy, Peter."

"I love you, Mom," I say. "You are the best mother I could have ever imagined." She smiles, brighter this time. She waves again. I repeat what I said, this time in Bisayan.

Mom's eyes flutter. I take it as a sign that she knows what I'm saying. She blows me a kiss.

"Goodbye, Mom," I whisper, before taking a deep breath, turning around, and walking to my car for the long drive back.

✦

Once at home, I sleep for the next twenty-four hours. I am exhausted and running a fever. But the next morning, March 27th, I feel a little better and get out of bed to brew my morning coffee. I take a sip, happy to taste its sugar and cream sweetness and feel its warmth seep into me. I stand, but the coffee does not stay down. I bend over and vomit, then grab a towel to clean the mess up.

This is strange, I am thinking. In a life of almost seventy years, I can remember vomiting only twice. I am woozy but start wobbling down the hall to the bedroom. Then I vomit again. This time, Mary rushes up to me. She doesn't say anything.

"I need to lie down," I say. "I'll be okay. I just need to lie down."

"No," she says firmly. "You're going to the ER."

Mary's decision saves my life.

✦

I remember walking with Mary into the ER at Tacoma General Hospital. I remember sitting down. I don't remember anything else.

"You went downhill quickly," Mary tells me months later. "When your heart failed, you screamed. It was the scariest sound I've ever heard." Mary pauses. "Your lungs were filling with fluid. All of your systems were shutting down. I'm minutes from losing you. Maybe for a moment I did lose you, and you came back. I'm not sure."

She looks away and takes a deep breath. "The ER doc, your condition, the situation is beyond his ability. I'm frustrated, scared. So I scream, 'We don't have time. Get me a goddamn pulmonary specialist, someone who can handle this. Now!'"

I chuckle. Mary is not a large woman, but she can be fierce and persistent, a tireless and sometimes joyful beater of brows. During our years together I've been the occasional target of some of my wife's ear-piercing screams.

"And so?" I ask, knowing the answer.

She stretches and stifles a yawn. "Why, a specialist shows up," Mary says.

"Of course."

"And he says you have a pulmonary edema accompanied by acute heart failure. It's the worst he's ever seen. He's going to intubate you and shoot you full of meds. He tells me it's the only thing that might save your life. But first he needs my permission."

"And then . . ."

"Go for it," she tells the doc.

I smile and nod. That sounds like Mary.

"Then I get curious," Mary says. "Doctor," she asks, "how many times have you done this before?" The doc answered "twice" and started walking toward me.

"And so, what happened?" I ask Mary.

"He turns and looks at me. 'They both died,' the doc says."

"But I didn't die," I say. "Dang, you saved my life again."

"It's what I do."

✦

According to Mary, I wake up in a hospital room three days later. But before then, I am floating in a vivid world of dreams. In one scene I am on a boat, fishing for snapper in the Sound. As soon as I land one, I scale it, fry it, and eat it.

In a later episode I am visiting with family and friends and meeting people I hadn't met but would meet later when I return to the flesh-and-blood world. That includes a lovely Ukrainian nurse with whom I share a vivid, lascivious, dream-state interlude.

This isn't so bad, I am thinking at the time. The doctors, nurses, and med techs make their rounds, with the doctors, in particular, carefully explaining my condition and the options available.

"Well," says my attending doc early in my recovery. "We now have to consider a heart transplant, or maybe a stent. These are possibilities you must consider."

He is solemn, and I nod solemnly. And although I don't say anything, I just hate the idea of being cut open. During my life I have never had even minor surgery. No tonsils removed. Nothing. This is a record I desperately want to keep.

Besides, I like the heart I was born with. It was wounded, not killed.

About a week into recovery, I have an epiphany. I suddenly remember that the heart is a muscle, which means that with enough good nutrition, exercise, and rest it can recover. And to everyone else's surprise, I am recovering. Quickly.

But I'm not surprised. The endless battery of tests tells me I'm on the way back. With each passing day, I grow more confident, almost giddy. *Surgeons, keep your damn scalpels away*, I want to scream. *Anesthesiologists, go away. Put someone else under, not me.*

My attending doc comes by as he always does. I've formed an opinion. I like him. He is a nice young man, highly competent, and a graduate of an excellent medical school. But he's by the book and probably won't accept what I'm about to tell him.

"Doc," I say calmly. "I won't need surgery." I explain the circumstances leading to my collapse: weeks of extreme depression and exhaustion, a serious illness. "My heart attack was caused by a perfect storm," I say. "And of course, under those circumstances, my heart collapsed. But those conditions are gone now. My mind is clear, relaxed, and right now my heart is using this time to repair itself, so . . ."

I pause and look at him, searching his face for a sign, maybe a skeptical grimace. But the doc is calm, scientifically distant, appropriately professional, no hint of a giveaway. That mind-body thing? Such New Agey nonsense, he's probably thinking. I don't think he believes it. But I do, so I plow forward.

"I know my body and mind," I say firmly. "I know what my heart's doing. It's healing."

He nods, and this time, it's his turn to not say a thing.

✦

Over the next two weeks I continue to improve and will soon be released. My doc has stopped talking about surgery. Instead, he now suggests that I go home with an IV and wear a defibrillator vest, which would spark my heart just in case it went south.

An earnest young sales rep comes in and fits me. He explains how this unwieldy, ill-fitting contraption works. I don't like it.

"Hmm," I say, while sneaking a "no way in hell" glance to Mary, who knows exactly what to do. I smile but don't say a word.

The earnest sales rep leaves just as my nurse practitioner, a wise and kind professional, walks in. She has been on this job for almost thirty years, and by now she is never surprised. The doctors, especially the younger ones, trust her and seek her advice.

I extend my left arm. She will be taking my blood pressure.

"Peter won't be needing the vest," Mary says firmly.

The nurse nods. "Normal," she says, then pauses. "Oh, and why?"

"His heart is coming back," Mary says firmly. "All the tests indicate he's almost normal."

"I'll tell the doctor," she says.

Later, Mary torpedoes the take-home IV. Time is short; I am scheduled for release the following day.

"I don't have the background to monitor an IV," she tells my nurse. Mary is adamant, focused, about to growl. "This is dangerous," she says. "Lunacy."

"I'll tell the doctor," the nurse replies.

My wife follows up with a coup de grace. "Besides, I feel a migraine coming on," she says, as she massages her temples. She doesn't, really, but she somehow persuades herself to vomit.

"I'll tell the doctor," the nurse says.

Mary's performance is so good it buys me an extra three days in the hospital, enough time for more good readings and test outcomes. It's also enough time for my attending doc to reconsider his IV proposal.

✦

When I am released, I am given a bag and a walker. The bag contains my medications and a date in July for a follow-up appointment. The vest and the IV are nowhere in sight.

More than a year later, I am still alive and doing well. From my admission to the ER to the day of my release, I received first-class medical care, for which I am thankful.

But here's what will stay with me, an indelible imprint for as long as I breathe: In my case, at least, the doctors and the medical staff listened to growling Mary and me. Others have told me that is not often the case.

✦

In my dream I return to the cemetery.

It is later in the day. The priest and the mourners are gone. I am alone in the mausoleum and whisper one more prayer for Mom and Dad. I stop in front of the niches containing the remains of many others from the old Seattle community. For whatever reason, a lot of Pinoys have chosen to be buried here.

I know these names: Bergano, De Los Santos, Acena, several others. These Pinoys have known each other for years. This mausoleum is the old community's neighborhood of the dead. Before I leave, I make sure to greet them all and wish them well.

I walk slowly toward my car. On this very sad day, I am smiling.

Years ago, I wrote a sentence about this very place: "Friends in life, they've chosen to be together again."

It was true then.

It is true today.

Rest well.

But for me, I tell myself: "Not yet," I whisper. "Not yet."

POSTSCRIPT TO
A HEART ATTACK

ary said that I died on March 27, 2019, that my heart
had failed. Same with my lungs and kidneys and
liver. As far as my condition, I have to admit that
this was genuinely impressive, the royal flush of bodily
system failures, my ticket seemingly punched to the
afterlife.

No wonder I flatlined.

"I was closing my eyes and praying, getting ready to say
goodbye," Mary told me later. She gulped and looked away.
"It was hard," she whispered.

"It was hard, I know," I said and held her hand.

She shuddered. "No, no, you don't know," she answered.

I paused. "You're right. I don't know."

Yet, despite my grim start, the docs at Tacoma General
somehow managed to save me. When I was in recovery,

there was some loose talk of having to cut me open. I begged them not to—the doctors, nurses, anyone with a white coat who walked into my room. For starters, I don't like knives of any kind. They scare me, and besides, I had lived almost sixty-nine years without surgery. This was a record I wanted to keep.

"My heart is fine," I explained to a skeptical young doctor. "It's a muscle, Doc, a muscle. It's gonna recover, I'm tellin' ya."

"We'll see," he said.

"There's a backstory to this."

The two weeks before my heart attack, I explained, were the most stressful of my life. I was battling bronchitis, exhaustion, depression. The son of two very good friends had just died. My mother was on the verge of dying. I was running a fever when I traveled to Seattle to spend the night at the hospital. A few days later and still very sick, I traveled to Seattle to say goodbye to Mom.

I stood at the doorway of my sister's house and waved at her in the living room. She waved back. I then said goodbye, first in English, then in Bisayan. Mom smiled, her dementia temporarily suspended. I turned around and got into my car for the forty-mile drive home.

"You shouldn't have done that," Mary scolded me later that day.

"I had to," I replied.

"No, you didn't."

Mary was right. A couple of days later my heart said, "Enough." It stopped. In retrospect, it should have been no surprise, really.

But three weeks after my heart attack, I was released from Tacoma General, cut free with a bag full of meds and a date for my first checkup. And for the next two months, Mary tended to me, making sure I did everything by the book. Then came the appointments with medical staff and doctors and an impressive battery of tests.

Everything was going well, the medical staff assured me, much better than anyone could have ever expected.

"How long will it take before I know I'm *really* out of the woods?" I asked.

"A year or so," my nurse said.

And indeed, half a year quickly passed, then nine months, then eleven—all without incident or even a hint of minor concern. It had all been going so smoothly, too smoothly for my comfort. Somewhere in the back of my mind was a doubt, which grew sharper and larger the closer I came to what would be the first anniversary of the day I died: March 27, 2020.

Would I make it to Saturday, March 28? That was the question I couldn't erase.

When March 27th arrived, it began like any COVID-triggered stay-at-home day. I smudged with tobacco and sage to my Mandan protectors tattooed on my right shoulder—Grandfather Oscar, the Contraries, and Eagle. I had learned to do this with my second wife, a Mandan, who performed her people's rituals and observed their traditions.

Then I worked out, ate a light breakfast, and caught up on the news. I chatted with Mary, then wrote. More news. Some dinner. More writing. More chatting with Mary. Then time for bed.

Nothing out of the ordinary, I told myself. Nothing at all to trigger my overblown fears.

In fact, I was so confident I would make it through the day that before turning in, I emailed my good friend, James.

At this time last year, I was dead. But I am still alive, so I think I will make it to the 28th. Gonna celebrate a minute after midnight.

My optimism was premature. The severe chills came first—hands and feet especially—then the out-of-control shaking and shortened breath. I looked at the clock—11:35.

"Damn," I whispered. "So close, so fuckin' close."

COVID or flu? I have no idea. With my compromised heart, it didn't make a difference. Either one would have killed me.

I prayed to my Mandan protectors and within minutes the warmth in my body began to return and the shaking suddenly stopped.

My mind churned. Mandans believe there are no accidents. Someone had sent this virus, an enemy, but who? I had no answer and was too tired to find out.

Mary, awakened by my ruckus, touched my forehead with the palm of her hand. She got out of bed and returned a few minutes later, carrying a coffee mug filled with hot water mixed with honey and lemon. By then the assault on my body was over.

"I'm okay," I said.

"Drink it anyway."

I took one sip, then another. The warm honey water was soothing, relaxing. I turned over on my side ready to sleep. But before I closed my eyes, I glanced at the clock: 12:01.

I took a deep breath. "Man, I've made it," I whispered.

EULOGY

Mother, about nine years ago, your advancing years formed a posse to kidnap your mind and lock it in a loop from which there is no escape. During this time I would visit, as I always have, and you'd smile and you'd speak not to me but to those who had died.

Of your brothers and sisters, your brave and persistent wartime generation, you were the only one left.

The last woman standing.

This is life as it has too often been. And even when you were alive, I have spent the last few years mourning your passing.

Knowing that, I wanted to create a song in prose, perhaps an opera that would have pleased Freddie Mercury.

For me, you are the best mother I could have ever imagined. This modest collection of anecdotes will help explain why.

When I think of you, a collage of memories crowds my mind. Of me at three listening to you play the piano and sing in Bisayan about how melancholy you were.

In truth, you could neither sing nor play the piano, but I could feel your sorrow. And how could I not? We were best friends, and I was your confidant.

Then a little later, when I was constipated and sitting on the stool, you poked your head inside the bathroom, your face etched in motherly concern.

"Don't push so hard," you solemnly said.

"Why not?"

"Your stomach will come out."

"Oh."

The next day you and Dad had some Filipino friends over, a mix of old-timers and newer arrivals like yourself. You were all in the living room, chatting, laughing, and munching on *lumpia*. Several times, I had groaned and pushed and groaned and pushed, but nothing had come out.

I was concerned. Maybe I'd gone too far.

I walked over to you, pulled down my pants, bent over and asked, "Did my stomach come out?"

"No, son," you casually replied, before kissing me on the head. "Now pull up your pants and go to the kitchen. Manang Pacing and I were just remembering life back home. She brought her lumpia, your favorite, the fat ones with chicken, and lettuce, and raisins."

Pacing nodded and smiled. "Just for you."

"Now get some before they're all gone."

You paused. "Hoy, and stop eating so much cheese."

Relieved, I pulled up my pants. And you and Pacing resumed chatting and laughing and munching on lumpia.

Just a day in the life.

As I loaded my plate with freshly cooked lumpias, I promised myself I would stop eating cheese.

Then there was the time—I think I was five—and you spanked me for some transgression I don't recall. Dad was the lord of discipline, an old-school cat who used a belt, twisted his waist, and followed through like Mickey at the plate. But for whatever reason he was gone that day, maybe to Chinatown to play cards and visit pals.

Whatever the reason, I knew I'd caught a break.

"You were bad," you said sternly.

No reply. Instead I looked down and flipped the switch to lip-quiver mode.

"Are you sorry?"

"Yes," I mumbled, head still down.

"Will you do it again?"

I shook my head.

"I still have to spank you."

"I know," I said sadly.

You raised your right hand and aimed a slap at my butt. "Ouch," I said, although it stung but didn't really hurt.

"Again."

"Ouch!" I screeched, although this one hurt even less.

"Now go to your room," you said.

Head still down, lower lip reliably quivering, I started walking to my room, wondering if my trove of tiny German and American soldiers, camped in separate shoeboxes, were ready for yet another epic showdown.

Then, on my seventh birthday, I was happy and full of expectations. Maybe a new cap gun, a train engine, or a cowboy hat, or if I lucked out, perhaps all three.

I blew out the candles. A round of applause.

Then you and Dad brought in boxes crammed with volumes of Funk and Wagnalls, the entire encyclopedic set.

"Read it," Dad said bluntly.

It was an order, and I nodded, trying to hide my disappointment.

Mom tousled my hair and kissed my forehead. "Happy birthday, son. Now finish your cake. You don't have to start reading today."

Eventually, out of boredom I suppose, I did start reading the encyclopedia. To my surprise, I found myself enjoying it, especially when I discovered new things, like the battles and the names of the generals of World War II. That meant my tiny American and German soldiers could now refight the Allied landing at Normandy.

More than sixty years later, I still have a passion for history, my first academic love. I am still curious about the "hows" and "whys" of significant events. Funk and Wagnalls and you and Dad gave me that gift, and your son thanks you.

ACT II

In 1972 I was no longer a child but a somewhat serious young man starting my second year of law school. That fall, though, the Uniform Commercial Code took a back seat to political organizing.

The drama of the next several weeks started quietly enough, an announcement by King County that a domed sports stadium would be built next to Chinatown. State of the art, or so its backers bragged, a sure-fire lure for big-time baseball and football franchises. The stadium would proclaim to the nation and the world that Seattle—then a drab and modest midsize city with a drab and modest reputation—had finally arrived.

The site was chosen because Chinatown residents were too poor and colored, too powerless—or so county officials thought.

The stadium would also drive up property values and rents, forcing the elderly to move out of a neighborhood they'd called home for forty years or more. Some were my dad's old cronies who'd left the Philippines and come to this land as young men. I knew many of them—their lives, their dingy roach-infested hot plate rooms, their poverty and diminished dreams.

In those days, Chinatown was a neighborhood of smoke-filled joints—a pool hall and a dive bar here, the Manila Café, the Victory Bath House, and a card room there. It wasn't much, but it was all the old Pinoys had left.

As a child, I knew all of these places and their patrons well. Mother, you did, too.

How could I not fight back? How could you not fight back? It was a sentiment shared by young Filipino and other Asian American activists, as well as many Chinatown residents.

We held community meetings; we organized. The local media noticed. Momentum built.

Earlier that year, I had asked Legal Services to intervene on behalf of the residents and persuaded several to serve as plaintiffs. We lost in court—no surprise given the potent political and economic winds pushing the project.

Reme Bacho, partially hidden, carrying the sign "Hum Bows Not Hot Dogs," 1972. Photo courtesy of Eugene M. Tagawa.

That left Plan B: Forget the Kingdome, I argued. It's a done deal. Instead, pressure local and federal agencies to cough up enough federally subsidized housing for Chinatown. That meant marching on the Seattle office of the Department of Housing and Urban Development.

After one of those meetings you said you'd be in the march.

"But," I said, knowing that what starts out peaceful can sometimes go south.

"Shh," you said. "Dad's friends, they're my friends, too. It's the least I can do."

And march is what you and hundreds of others did on November 12, from Chinatown to the HUD office on Second Avenue. An iconic photo captured you near the front of the march, stylishly dressed that brisk, breezy morning—from

The author making a point to HUD officials, 1972. Photo courtesy of Eugene M. Tagawa.

your winter coat to your fur hat, like you were going to mass at Immaculate.

You were also carrying a sign: "Hum Bows Not Hot Dogs."

Inside the building, we crowded into a meeting room, where I sat across the table from nervous HUD officials dressed in blue and gray polyester suits. In my best "mau mau" imitation, I kept jamming my thumb on the table, demanding that the federal government pay attention to the housing needs of Chinatown's poor.

And within a few years, federal and local funds started pouring into Chinatown, the money going to refurbish old units and expand the stock of subsidized housing.

That meant that the old Pinoys, your old Pinoys, wouldn't have to move. And they could live out their lives in decent

The author, in wool cap, huddling before the march with other protest leaders in Chinatown, 1972. Photo courtesy of Eugene M. Tagawa.

apartments—not hot plate rooms—in living conditions much better than they'd known.

For you, the Chinatown march was just the start. You kept going as part of a group that founded the International Drop-In Center, which provided services for Chinatown's elderly and poor. And you stayed for more than thirty years. I don't how many you helped apply for citizenship, get veterans benefits, or apply for Social Security, but more than a thousand sounds about right.

You were their advocate, their angel who spoke English well enough to say, "I want to speak to your supervisor."

Then there was the time I came home to find two women, mid-thirties' Filipinas I didn't know, sleeping on the living room floor.

"Mom," I said. "Um, who are these . . ."

"That's Esther; the shorter one, that's Stella."

The two looked up. Shorter Stella rubbed her eyes.

"This is my eldest, Peter," you said, as I bussed you on the cheek. "He's going to be an attorney."

I waved. They shyly waved back.

"Now, go get something to eat."

"Um, Mom . . ."

"They left the Philippine Consulate a few days ago, claiming abuse and poor working conditions, and they had nowhere to go. It's in the papers. No other Filipinos would take them in. Too dangerous. So Father Ocana asks me, and I say why not."

You shrugged.

"How can you say no to a priest?"

"What did Dad say?"

Dad was seated at the kitchen table, sipping coffee and reading the *Seattle Times*. "Hmph," he grunted without looking up.

"He didn't say no," you said with a smile.

And, I thought, *How could Dad say no to you?*

"He never does," I said.

Another smile.

Your decision meant that you and Dad could be facing serious consequences. You had property in the Philippines, family too, that the Philippine dictator Ferdinand Marcos could have moved against. But you were the only one in this community who went ahead, and you dragged Dad with you.

Marcos was ruthless and brutal, but he sure knew how to suck a teat. That meant keeping the Americans happy and the money pipeline open—no bad press, the appearance of reform, fascism with a smiling brown face.

The story Stella and Frances told wasn't part of Manila's sunny narrative.

Should they be forced to return to the Philippines for leaving the consulate and violating their work visas, they would have been in danger for embarrassing the regime. That meant keeping them here—at all costs. During the following months, there would be immigration hearings, petitions for asylum, and your old standby—marriage to old Filipino men who also happened to be US citizens. You'd arranged the last one, thanks to your deep pool of Drop-In Center clients who were old Filipino men who also happened to be US citizens.

In the end, Frances and Stella got married and stayed put, and Stella and her soon-to-be dead citizen husband even bought a house. Both of the women had you to thank.

And I thank you as well for this crystalline moment of moral clarity. As your son, I have never been prouder.

ACT III

One late October Sunday, before you'd lapsed into darkness, I came by for a visit. You were seated at the kitchen table sipping tea and reading the voters pamphlet.

I kissed you on the head and joined you at the table. You smiled.

"I always vote for Democrats," you said evenly.

"Why?"

"They help little people."

You picked up the pamphlet and slowly turned a page.

"Like us," you said, without looking up.

ENCORE

In my mind, there you are, Mom, playing the piano and singing your sad Bisayan song—a little off-key and missing a note or two.

My dearest wish is to see and to hear you sing and play the piano.

Again.

Tanya Sinkovits

ABOUT THE AUTHOR

Peter Bacho is the author of six books: *Cebu, Dark Blue Suit, Boxing in Black and White, Nelson's Run, Entrys*, and *Leaving Yesler. Cebu* won the 1992 American Book Award, and *Dark Blue Suit* won the Murray Morgan Prize and a Washington State Governor's Writers Award in 1998. His fiction, nonfiction, and screenplays have continued to earn wide acclaim.

As a child, Bacho lived in Seattle's blue-collar and multi-ethnic Central Area. He was the first in his family to graduate from high school, then college, and finally law school. He earned two law degrees from the University of Washington, in 1974 and 1981, and was later a staff attorney for the US Ninth Circuit Court of Appeals. During this time he was also an editorial contributor to the *Christian Science Monitor*, where he specialized on Philippine politics and covered issues ranging from politics to war. He is currently an adjunct professor at The Evergreen State College–Tacoma Campus.